# England's Jane:

## The Story of

# Jane Austen

# England's Jane:

## The Story of

# Jane Austen

Juliane Locke

**MORGAN
REYNOLDS**
**PUBLISHING**
Greensboro, North Carolina

# WORLD WRITERS

CHARLES DICKENS

JANE AUSTEN

STEPHEN KING

RALPH ELLISON

ROBERT FROST

**ENGLAND'S JANE: THE STORY OF JANE AUSTEN**

Copyright © 2006 by Juliane Locke

Library of Congress Cataloging-in-Publication Data

Locke, Juliane, 1959-
  England's Jane: the story of Jane Austen / Juliane Locke.— 1st ed.
  p. cm.
  Includes bibliographical references and index.
  ISBN-13: 978-1-931798-82-2 (lib. bdg.)
  ISBN-10: 1-931798-82-6 (lib. bdg.)
  1. Austen, Jane, 1775-1817—Juvenile literature. 2. Novelists, English—
19th century—Biography—Juvenile literature. I. Title.
  PR4036.L63 2006
  823'.7—dc22

                              2005026279

Printed in the United States of America
First Edition

For Tim and Jordan with love

# Contents

*Jane Austen.* (National Portrait Gallery, London)

# ONE

# A Rectory Childhood

In the summer of 2002, inhabitants of a Scottish castle came across a set of three leather-bound books that had been published in 1813. Suspecting the books might be worth something to collectors, the castle owners got an appraisal. Auctioneers in Edinburgh estimated the volumes would probably sell for the U.S. equivalent of $18,000. But when the day of the auction arrived, collectors from around the world came to bid on these books. When the gavel came down on the final bid, the three-volume first edition of Jane Austen's *Pride and Prejudice* had sold for $62,500.

For a struggling writer little known in her own time, Jane Austen has been remembered and revered beyond reasonable expectation. While the six novels she wrote never earned her a fraction of what those first editions sold for at auction, today Austen is considered not only the most ingenious English novelist of her day, but among the greatest writers of all time. Much of her lasting popularity is because her novels, written nearly two hundred years ago, are still relevant today. Austen's focus on the intricacies of human relationships, the details of love and romance, and the interactions between family members keeps her work as fresh today as it was when it was written.

Unfortunately for posterity, Austen did not leave behind an autobiography or even a journal. Not much is known about the thoughts of the woman behind the novels. We do know that she lived a quiet life, presumably possessing the social reserve and well-mannered conformity of a model British subject. Yet she expressed in her novels a brilliant, original mind and witty portrayals of absurdity in all its manifestations. Austen was born with the gift of humor and developed in her lifetime a profound insight into human nature. These qualities, combined with a formidable writing talent, allowed her to turn the novel of manners into a vehicle for literary genius.

Jane Austen's life began modestly. "We now have another girl," George Austen wrote in a letter announcing her birth, "a present plaything for her sister Cassy and a future companion." Jane was born on December 16, 1775, the seventh child in the family. The only other girl, Cassandra, was almost three. Jane's birth was one of many things happening at the crowded Austen house-

*This late-eighteenth-century view of the Hampshire countryside gives a sense of the quiet rural atmosphere of Jane's childhood.* (King George III Topographical Collection, London)

hold nine days before Christmas that year. In the same letter, her father gave equal time to reporting farming events and other activities, for he was not only a scholar, a tutor, and a clergyman for two parishes, but also a gentleman farmer (one who manages but doesn't necessarily labor).

Austen's parents were bright, educated, and practical, teaching their children to esteem literature and language no less than manners and morality. Jane's mother was from a family of the aristocracy—the highest social class in England. By choosing to marry George Austen, a descendant of merchants, she had married beneath her class and thus had functionally placed herself and her children among the gentry—a step down for a person of her background. But Cassandra Austen was a down-to-earth woman and no stranger to hard work. She managed the house and garden, supervised the servants, and kept a mother's eye on her own children as well as her husband's boarding pupils.

Yet while Mrs. Austen's social class did not interfere with her work, it might explain her approach to mothering small children. When Jane, whom the family called Jenny, was just weaned, Mrs. Austen took her to stay at a cottage on a neighboring farm, where the woman of the house was paid a fee to be a temporary mother. Jane was not exactly abandoned; one or both of her parents visited almost every day. Some days, Jane would be brought to her own home for a visit. But she was made to reside at the farm until she was old enough to run about and express herself verbally.

The practice of sending away babies to be cared for by others was common only among upper-class families, and all of Mrs. Austen's eight children underwent the same routine in babyhood. Like her siblings, Jane spent her early childhood with a family known as Littleworth, who lived at Cheesedown Farm. There she was cared for until she could return home to join the talking and walking ranks of the clever and talented Austen children.

All of Cassandra Austen's children survived infancy, which was somewhat exceptional for the times. They were generally healthy, with the exception of George, the second Austen child, born in 1766. He too spent his early years at Cheesedown Farm, where it became evident that he was mentally ill, exhibiting what his mother called fits. "My poor little George is come to see me today," Mrs. Austen wrote in a letter when her son was about five. "He seems pretty well, tho' he had a fit lately; it was near a twelvemonth since he had one before, so was in hopes they had left him, but must not flatter myself so now." Mrs. Austen had to face up to the truth about her son, which she understood would mean losing him; abnormal children were generally sent away.

*This sketch of the rectory at Steventon was made by Jane's niece, Anna Lefroy.* (Jane Austen House, Chawton)

George could not speak normally and struggled vainly to express himself. His specific disorder was never recorded, but at the age of six, because his fits had begun to adversely affect his siblings, little George was sent to live with a distant uncle who was paid to provide board and care. George would never return to live with his family and would never again be included in the Austen family's lives or letters. It was as if he had died.

The eldest Austen offspring, James, was already at Oxford when Jane was born. Yet even with two brothers missing from the Steventon rectory where Jane grew up, there was no shortage of boys around the house. In addition to the four brothers who were still at home in the two-story cottage, there were usually two or three of her father's pupils living in the household at any given time. Because family, boarders, and servants filled the house to capacity, Jane and Cassandra, the only girls, had to share a room. This arrangement suited them perfectly, for they were very close—they remained best friends all of their lives.

The two sisters did everything together. Jane was apparently much closer to Cassandra than she was to her own mother. When it came time for the older girl to go away to school, Jane refused to be separated from her sister. "If Cassandra's head had been going to be cut off," Mrs. Austen remarked, "Jane would insist on sharing her fate."

Jane's stubbornness apparently paid off. In 1782, with both parents' blessings, the six-year-old climbed into the carriage that transported her and Cassandra to their first school experience, their first adventure away from home by themselves. They would not be entirely surrounded by strangers; their cousin, Jane Cooper, was a fellow student and the school was run by Mrs. Cawley, a distant relative of Mrs. Austen.

After settling into their Oxford boarding school surroundings, the girls were uprooted again when Mrs. Cawley decided to move the whole school to Southampton. Jane and Cassandra packed up and resettled at the second location—a move that would bring tragedy.

At the new school there was an outbreak of severe sickness. Both Austen girls and their cousin were infected with a highly contagious and potentially deadly illness known as the putrid fever, or typhus. The ailment had stricken several students in the school, but for some reason Mrs. Cawley did not contact the children's parents.

All three girls might have died in Southampton had it not been for young Jane Cooper, who wrote home and told her mother they were sick. Mrs. Cooper shared the news with Mrs. Austen, and the two mothers traveled to the school to bring the girls home. Little Jane grew steadily worse; they feared she would not make it, but eventually both Austen girls and their cousin pulled through. Sadly, however, Mrs. Cooper caught typhus from her daughter and died.

Three years passed before Cassandra and Jane left home for a second time. This time they didn't travel far.

*The town of Reading, where the Austen girls attended the Abbey School in the 1780s, had developed as a bustling clothing-manufacturing center and would have felt far more sophisticated than any place the girls had experienced before.* (King George III Topographical Collection, London)

In 1785, when Jane was ten years old, the Austen girls arrived at the Abbey School in Reading, which would serve as home and school for the next two years.

The Abbey School was conducted in a twelfth-century gatehouse, a structure with an archway where gatekeepers once kept an eye on the people, carts, and livestock passing in and out of the abbey grounds. To the girls it was an exotic building, not the sort of thing they would see in the farmlands where the Austens resided. The school also made use of a two-story home adjacent to the gatehouse. In this strange new place,

Jane could wander in an old-fashioned garden and gaze down upon the ruins of the centuries-old abbey, a fallen Benedictine structure once among the largest and richest in England.

Jane's young imagination was free to embrace the haunted flavor of this school set among ruins, in a landscape that offered all the excitements of the Gothic novels popular at the time. A human skeleton was discovered under the Abbey walls. A severed hand was found, all shriveled and dry, and thought to be a saint's relic. Ghost stories were told about the dead King Henry I, whose remains—minus the eyes—were buried close by the school.

The woman in charge of the Abbey School called herself Mrs. Latournelle, though she was not the Frenchwoman her name implied. Her real name was Sarah Hackett, but she went by Latournelle at the suggestion of school officials, who hoped to enhance her respectability and appeal. Her main distinguishing feature was an artificial leg made of cork—though she would never say how she had lost the real one.

In Jane's time, girls were not expected to study as rigorously as boys; classical languages and other topics were not taught to them. The fact that Jane and Cassandra went to school at all was evidence of their parents' liberal thinking, for in those days money spent on educating girls was generally seen as money thrown away. After all, women could not have careers, participate in trade, or hold an office. They were groomed to be wives and mothers. If they could not find husbands, then they might work as governesses, but only a poor girl would stoop so low.

Mrs. Latournelle was remembered as being kind to the girls and providing ample free time in which students were left to themselves. When class was in session, the one topic Mrs. Latournelle seems to have spoken upon with the greatest authority and enthusiasm was the theater. Jane and the others heard a great deal about actors and plays, and performed in scenes, an activity Jane happily pursued with her family during much of her life.

The Abbey School experience ended when Jane was twelve years old. After the Austen parents realized how much free time the girls had at school, it was decided that their time would be better spent at home. For Jane and Cassandra, boarding school days were over. They came home for good, and ever after Jane would depend upon books and conversation to educate herself.

Jane was an avid reader, and at home she was able to read the latest English novels with as much freedom as she read Shakespeare and the Bible. Not every daughter of a clergyman would have been allowed to do so, for in those days novels were frowned upon as a potential threat to anyone's morality, but most especially the tender morals of young women. Characters in popular novels were likely to be driven by lust or romantic love. Although there were moralistic novels published, the ones that were most widely read did not contain modest

*This 1801 miniature depicts Jane's father, the Reverend George Austen.*

characters who behaved themselves. Novels were also frowned upon because they were sometimes written by women, who at the time were socially undervalued and, in general, not considered either sufficiently intellectual nor formally educated enough to create any writing of literary merit. Nevertheless, novels were popular, especially with young Jane and her family.

Mr. Austen kept a well-stocked library—hundreds of volumes—and he welcomed his children to enjoy any book. Jane made continuous use of his collection, though she did not read novels to the exclusion of other books. She loved keeping up with the admired thinkers of her day and accepted the suggestions made by her father and her two scholarly brothers, James and Henry, who helped guide her early reading choices.

*A silhouette of Jane's aristocratic mother, Cassandra Austen. Silhouette was a very popular art form during Jane's life.*

Along with the many books she read, what helped shape Jane's remarkable mind was her family. The Austens feasted on words. They enjoyed reading, rhyming, and riddling as well as critiquing literature. Language, skillfully manipulated, was their primary source of entertainment, and the family read aloud to each other, both the writings of published authors and the works they composed for one another's enjoyment.

Mrs. Austen often penned witty poems to gently and humorously drive a point home. On behalf of her husband's pupils who complained about the loud weather vane outside the house, she wrote a poem that concluded: "It whines and it groans and makes such a noise / That it greatly disturbs two unfortunate boys /

Who hope you will not be displeased when they say / If they don't sleep at night they can't study by day."

Composing messages in verse form was one of the ways the Austen family shared their sense of humor and wit. So, with a ready audience for her comic genius, Jane began her writing career at an early age, creating spoofs to make her family laugh.

# TWO

## A Comic Writer

T he youngest child in a busy household, Jane
Austen was quiet in crowds or with strangers,
but her charming and funny personality
emerged when she was with those she loved best—her
family. When she and Cassandra returned from school,
they spent their time helping their mother with the
house, reading, sewing, drawing, painting, or—Jane's
favorite activity—writing. With pen and paper, quiet
Jane was able to release the thoughts and jokes that
sprang from her active mind.

Jane's father, George Austen, was a kindly, quiet man
who loved his children very much. He listened to them
patiently and encouraged them in everything they tried.
It is hard to imagine such a parent becoming angry when
he discovered, as George did, that Jane had been

writing herself into the marriage register at his church.

"The banns of marriage," Jane wrote in the ledger, "between Henry Frederick Howard Fitzwilliam of London and Jane Austen of Steventon." Jane believed that when "Fitz" was attached before a surname, it indicated the illegitimate offspring of royalty. Lesser rank was acceptable to Jane as well, since she did not stop at one husband. "Mr. Edmund Arthur William Mortimer of Liverpool and Jane Austen of Steventon were married in this church," she wrote on another page. Her third fictional husband was simply "Jack Smith," with no address.

The rituals of courtship and marriage were central to the society in which Jane Austen lived. Making a good marriage was extremely important, and young women were raised to think always of winning a husband. It is not surprising, then, that so much of Austen's writing should focus on the relationship between men and women. She particularly enjoyed investigating and dramatizing the complicated rules that governed courtship.

At the age of fifteen, with a delight in the ridiculous, Jane wrote a spoof on the history of England, which, in her experience, had been written with entirely too much focus on dates and on men. To remedy this imbalance, Jane took historic figures and events and reinvented them according to her own sense of poetic justice and humor, spotlighting female figures. Lady Jane Grey was queen of England for nine days before being dethroned, tried for treason, and executed in 1554. Yet Jane Austen did not make her a hero but portrayed her as so vain about her classical education that she busily composed sentences in Latin and Greek on her way to the scaffold. On the title page, Jane explained gravely that her version of history would have very few dates. She read it out loud to the amusement of her family.

Jane enjoyed reading novels in which there were excessively tearful love scenes and swooning females; the books were not intended to be funny, but Jane always laughed at rational people behaving in irrational ways. Among her earliest writings is a novel in letters called *Love and Friendship,* in which she spoofs the dizzy heroines of popular romance novels. An affected character named Sophia swoons herself literally to death in Jane's story. And though Sophia is dying, she makes the time to counsel a close friend. "Beware of swoons Dear Laura," Sophia advises, digressing to remark briefly that frenzy, on the other hand, may have health benefits. "Run mad as often as you chose," Sophia says, "but do not faint."

While Jane's witty humor flowed freely in her writing, she was more restrained in her social life and often shy around strangers. Although she showed enormous energy, bordering on wildness, in her youth, Jane never shamed her family. Her earliest characters were scandalous indeed—they murdered, eloped, forged, lied, and stole. But dutiful Jane minded her manners.

In her letters to Cassandra, Jane often expressed herself in a hilarious and unchecked manner. "You ex-

*Cassandra's watercolor illustrations of Jane's* History of England. (The British Library, London)

press so little anxiety about my being murdered under the Ashe Park Copse [a copse is a woods on an estate] by Mrs. Hulbert's servant," Jane wrote in one letter, "that I have a great mind not to tell you whether I was or not."

Jane was encouraged in her imagination by Eliza, a cousin on her father's side. Eliza had been raised in India and then married a French count to gain the lofty title Madame la Comtesse de Feuillide. When Jane was eleven, Countess Eliza arrived at the Austen home with her baby son in tow. They had left Eliza's husband behind in France—the marriage was one made for social advancement, not for love—and Eliza was traveling with her

*The beautiful and lively Eliza de Feuillide helped cultivate Jane's creative tendencies when she came to live with her cousins, the Austens, in the 1790s.*

mother. She would quickly become a favorite and valued member of the extended Austen family.

When Eliza began visiting the Austen family, she found Jane, the young writer, both hilarious and bright. The two became friends, as Jane greatly admired her scandalous cousin. What satisfaction it must have given a wickedly funny girl like Jane to have in the family circle someone who boasted of adventures the upright Austens could hardly imagine. Eliza could tell firsthand stories of the palace of Versailles and the French aristocracy she had married into. She had been at the court of King Louis XVI and his infamous queen, Marie Antoinette, though she probably did not know them personally. Versailles was legendary for its excess, and Marie Antoinette was quickly becoming a symbol for the corruption that plagued the French court. Eliza had a quick wit and could tell riotously entertaining stories about the strange-seeming customs of the French.

## Marie Antoinette

Christened Maria Antonia Josepha Johanna, the Austrian archduchess who became the tragic French queen grew up in a privileged household—her father, Francis I, was the Holy Roman Emperor, and her mother, Empress Maria Theresa, was head of the Hapsburg dynasty, one of the most powerful families in Europe. Because she was the fifteenth of sixteen children, it was not expected that Maria Antonia would be needed to make a political marriage for

*Marie Antoinette, wife of Louis XVI of France.*

her family. She was a pretty child but preferred dancing to schooling and had trouble mastering the several languages expected of royalty.

Her life took a fateful turn when Austria and France signed a peace treaty that needed to be sealed with a marriage, and Maria Antonia was the only daughter available. In 1770, at the age of fourteen, she was married to the grandson of the French king, Louis XV, and became Marie Antoinette.

Marie Antoinette's new husband was named Louis XVI, king of France, when his grandfather died in 1774 and he ascended to the throne. The young couple did not have a happy marriage, and Louis's ineptness as king increased the tension. Despite the treaty, relations between France and Austria remained strained, and Marie Antoinette was often viewed with suspicion because of her foreign birth. She did not help her reputation by assembling a group of friends better known for their interest in parties and gambling than the increasingly perilous political situation. As Marie Antoinette purchased new dresses and jewels and gave elegant balls at the magnificent palace of Versailles, the economy of France teetered on the edge of bankruptcy and people went hungry in the streets. Oblivious to their growing resentment, the young queen continued to indulge in whatever took her fancy. Vicious rumors began to spread that Marie Antoinette was an adulterer and that she was plotting with Austria against France. She soon became a scapegoat for the misery of the French people.

*The revolutionaries guillotined Marie Antoinette in 1793.*

The explosion happened in 1789 when a mob took control of the Bastille (a large prison) and began the process of ending the rule of the French monarchy. As the Revolution continued, Louis and his family tried to flee but were captured and returned to Paris, where they were imprisoned in 1792. Louis was tried for treason and executed in January 1793. Marie Antoinette and her two surviving children (two others had died before the Revolution began) remained in prison until the former queen was brought to trial on October 14, 1793. After a perfunctory trial, she was sentenced to death the next day. On October 16, 1793, she was executed by guillotine. Her son died in prison in 1795. Her daughter was allowed to return to Austria, where she lived in exile until her death in 1851.

In her lifetime, Marie Antoinette was seen as a symbol of the excess and heartlessness of the French monarchy. More recently, she has come to be seen as a semi-tragic figure, a victim of circumstances she could hardly comprehend.

In Eliza were all the behaviors that Jane would never emulate, but which she would have her early comic characters positively flaunt. Eliza likely helped fire Jane's early writing imagination, providing lively, first-hand information about a glittering, scandalous world that existed outside the modest rectory of Steventon.

When Jane was fourteen, two of her brothers were already serving in the British Royal Navy when there was an uprising in France that shook the world. Inspired by the revolution that had taken place in the American colonies at the time of Jane's birth, the French Revolution in 1789 overthrew the monarchy and made way for republican rule. The beautiful queen about whom Eliza had told stories was executed at the guillotine in 1793, as was her husband. Thousands of people were killed in a bloody purge that sent shock waves across Europe.

Eliza had married into an old French family, which made her part of the now-targeted privileged class. In 1794, her husband was executed by the guillotine. Eliza, accompanied by her servant woman, fled to England, narrowly escaping with her life. She arrived at Steventon widowed and destitute. There are no letters recording Jane's thoughts about the tragedy, but she would be aware that her bold cousin had shown incredible resourcefulness, and that Eliza's perfect French, together with her determination and wits, was what allowed her to escape death or imprisonment in France.

The same year Eliza's husband was executed, Mr. Austen bought Jane a beautiful mahogany writing desk for her nineteenth birthday. Jane put the desk to immediate use, writing a story about a wild and wicked

*This pen-and-ink sketch shows the writing desk where Austen wrote both her famous novels and many of her letters.* (North Wind Picture Archive)

heroine named Lady Susan. Eliza may have been the inspiration for this character.

The humor young Jane Austen expressed in such exaggerated terms was to become more sophisticated over time, and began to include serious statements, particularly about the plight of women and the importance of the novel, which was emerging as a mostly female genre. In 1798, when Austen was twenty-three years old, she began a manuscript called *Catherine* (it would be revised and published much later as *Northanger Abbey*). In it, she wrote that the novel is "a work in which the greatest powers of the mind are displayed" along with the "most thorough knowledge of human nature." Austen added that in a novel one sees that "the liveliest effusions of wit and humor are conveyed to the world in the best-chosen language."

While defending the novel, Austen also made fun of the way women were depicted in popular novels. She included in her work shrewd observations about the plight of smart women, pointing slyly to the practical benefits of appearing to be stupid. Austen suggested that women seeking husbands did best by hiding their intelligence, to better flatter men into believing themselves the superior sex.

"Where people wish to attach, they should always be ignorant. To come with a well-informed mind, is to come with the inability of administering to the vanity of others," Austen wrote. "A woman especially, if she have the misfortune of knowing anything, should conceal it as well as she can." In her typical ironic humor, Austen makes her point: "Imbecility in females is a great enhancement to their personal charms."

In her personal correspondences, Austen could as easily be self-effacing, admitting to her own dullness: "Expect a most agreeable letter, for not being overburdened with subject (having nothing at all to say), I shall have no check upon my genius from beginning to end." On yet another occasion she wrote her sister, "There! I may now finish my letter and go hang myself, for I am sure I can neither write nor do anything which will not appear insipid to you after this." Austen seemed constantly aware of her writing, even when it was just a letter—and she wrote many letters.

*Cassandra captured a bit of Jane's contemplative nature in this unusual yet beautifully composed watercolor sketch from 1804.* (Collection of the three great-grandsons of Admiral Sir Francis Austen)

Many of Austen's letters were to her sister, Cassandra, and they reveal not only Austen's thoughts about life, politics, and writing but also more practical matters: the latest social news, recipes, and clothing fashions. Cassandra saved almost all of her sister's correspondence but destroyed a few letters—most likely ones with content too private to risk discovery. Still, the remaining letters give us a window into the life of the woman who found her freedom on the page.

# THREE

# A Home in the Country

"We shall have a most brilliant party & a great deal of amusement, the house full of company and frequent balls," Eliza wrote one winter, urging a young female relative to join the Austen family for Christmas festivities. One of the Austen brothers had fitted up the barn like a real theater, and there would be costumes fashioned for the occasion. Eliza had a lead role and was excited by all the fun there was to be had at the Austen household.

The play they performed in the barn that winter was funny and racy, one in which young people face conflicts with parents about arranged marriages, elopements, and romantic conspiracies. The play was no doubt a thrill to young Jane Austen—it was only lacking a few murders, suicides, or missing limbs for her taste.

All through girlhood and into her early twenties, Austen didn't have to go far for entertaining society. The Steventon rectory and those who visited there or lived under its roof made Austen's life full and interesting—whether it was theater in the barn, the recitation of original verses, or a reading of her latest comedy at the fireside. Conversations could be lively among the articulate Austen siblings. Cassandra was the artist, while James and Henry were the scholars. Frank and Charles were navy men, and Edward was in the process of becoming a wealthy gentleman.

Ever since early childhood, Austen had observed her brother Edward living two lives, being away from the family for longer and longer periods of time in order to visit with a wealthy, childless couple by the name of

*This silhouette shows Edward Austen being presented by his father to his adoptive parents, the wealthy Mr. and Mrs. Thomas Knight, from whom he would eventually inherit a substantial fortune.* (Jane Austen House, Chawton)

Knight. Distant relatives of the Austens, the Knights loved Edward and wanted to adopt him as their heir. Though it was hard for the family to lose a son, they knew that Edward (who eventually took the name Knight) had the opportunity to increase his standing and personal fortune. Even after he moved to the Knights' estate in Kent, Edward remained a part of the Austen family and saw them often.

Austen admired her siblings and was bound to them not only by sparkling wit and literary leanings but a sensible rootedness. Living as they did in the remote countryside, the Austens were grounded in the seasons, the weather, the livestock, and the crops. It was important to keep up the day-to-day work, making sure bread was baked, beer was brewed, the garden tended, and root vegetables stored away for winter. No matter how lofty the wit, banter, and book discussions, survival demanded the Austens remain firmly planted in the practical.

While every household had to make or raise most of its own food, the Austen household was distinguished for being the first in the village to produce potatoes, then considered an exotic vegetable. The Austens would have eaten food that was almost entirely provided by the farm and garden—from eggs and carrots to milk and ham. She reported on pigs in one of her letters, as casually as if

Opposite: *Edward Austen around the time of his grand tour of Europe. During Jane Austen's time, most educated, wealthy, young British noblemen took a grand tour, which could last from a few months to eight years. During the tour, young men learned about the politics, culture, art, and antiquities of neighboring countries.* (Jane Austen House, Chawton)

she were speaking of women's fashions. If there was bacon on her plate, she probably knew which pig it came from and on what day the animal had been slaughtered.

Life on a working farm was not physically demanding for the Austen girls—servants did most of the work, both indoor and outdoor chores, so there was plenty of leisure time for Jane to read. In 1798, Mr. Austen picked up the latest novel by Sir Egerton Bridges, and twenty-three-year-old Jane took the opportunity to joke about her own reading habits.

"We have got *Fitz-Albini*," she wrote to Cassandra. "Father has bought it against my private wishes, for it does not quite satisfy my feelings that we should purchase the only one of Egerton's works of which his family are ashamed. That these scruples, however, do not at all interfere with my reading it, you will easily believe."

Austen had eclectic tastes and seemed delighted to read any novel she could get her hands on. These included Gothic works such as *The Castle of Wolfenbach, Mysterious Warnings, The Necromancers of the Black Forest,* and *Horrid Mysteries*. While she favored classics such as *Tom Jones* and *Tristram Shandy,* the most lurid of her reading was *The Monk,* a novel that included incest, rape, and necrophilia.

During the eighteenth century, the novel was still an emerging form. As the middle class expanded, more people learned—and had the leisure time—to read. Their demand for entertainment fueled a publishing

# The Gothic Novel

**P**erhaps the most famous Gothic novel is Mary Shelley's *Franken-stein* (1818). It features many of the devices common to the genre, including a mysterious setting, people who are not what they seem to be, and elements of the supernatural. Gothic novels were popular during the late eighteenth and early nineteenth centuries, terrifying readers with the plight of beautiful young women thrust into strange circumstances. These women are often rescued by handsome men with dark or shadowy pasts.

Jane Austen's *Northanger Abbey,* not published until after her death in 1817, was a satirical take on this genre—a fact that may have delayed its publication, since Gothic novels were so popular. In *Northanger Abbey* (originally titled *Catherine*), Austen's title character is invited to an estate and, expecting to find it dark and mysterious like the ones in the books she read, is surprised to find the place clean, bright, and friendly. Still, Catherine's overactive imagination convinces her there is danger all about, and Austen uses her character's fear to jokingly suggest that so much reading could indeed influence a young woman's mind.

boom. Writers—many of them women—churned out books featuring the romance and drama readers had come to expect and enjoy. "Serious" literature was scarce by contrast, and associated with writers such as Daniel Defoe (*Robinson Crusoe,* 1719) and Henry Fielding (*Tom Jones,* 1749).

When a Mrs. Martin, who was opening a subscription library, assured Jane Austen that the book collection was "not to consist only of novels, but of every kind of literature," she was amused. No one would ever have to apologize to Austen for possessing an abundance of novels. She wrote to Cassandra, "She might have spared this pretension to our family, who are great novel readers and not ashamed of being so."

Reading was an excellent way for someone like Jane Austen—who never left England—to learn about the larger world. An Austen relative, describing England's rural society of the times, observed that "a rector [such as Austen's father] who chanced to be a gentleman and a scholar found himself superior to his chief parishioners in information and manners, and became a sort of center of refinement and politeness." The neighborhood scholar was often called upon as an authority to settle any number of questions. Mr. Austen was once asked a geography question. "You know all about these sort of things," the man said to Jane's father. "Do tell us. Is Paris in France or is France in Paris?"

In addition to many novels and books of poetry, a book that made the rounds at the Austen home and created lively discussion had to do with landscape aesthetics. William Gilpin's *Lakes Tour,* published in 1786, helped set an aesthetic standard that was to influence the way educated people viewed and altered their landscape. Gilpin was an admirer of landscape painting and came to have strong beliefs about what made for good subject matter. Not content to let nature be the artist, Gilpin explained that any view worthy of being reproduced in a work of art—a picture—was worthy of being considered picturesque and should be treated accordingly. This meant making improvements to bring the view into accord with Gilpin's idea of what was beau-

*This aquatint engraving of a ruin in Basingstoke, England, gives an idea of the "picturesque" landscape aesthetic promoted by William Gilpin. For Gilpin, texture and composition were important factors. The texture should be without obvious straight lines. The composition should work as a unified whole, incorporating a dark foreground and a brighter focal point. A ruined abbey or castle would add a visual weight to the view. While Gilpin believed that nature was good at producing textures and colors, he also thought it rarely produced the perfect composition. Some extra help from the artist, perhaps in the form of a carefully placed tree, was usually required.* (King George III Topographical Collection, London)

tiful. The popularity of Gothic novels was reflected in the tendency for attractive landscapes to feature the ruins of an old church or similar structure—usually constructed out of new materials and then painstakingly deconstructed to achieve the desired effect.

It would be natural for Austen to feel surprised and disappointed when she read that Gilpin thought little of her own neighborhood; he found nothing picturesque in her native landscape, nothing worthy of an artistic rendering. Having studied the principals of this popular aesthetic, Austen would make comic reference to the picturesque in her novels—not to mock the concept itself but the extremes to which people took the idea.

Her own parents applied their characteristic practicality when making improvements to their grounds, which they did during most of the three decades they lived at Steventon. "Our improvements have advanced very well," Austen wrote to her sister about a landscaping project. "The bank along the elm walk is sloped down for the reception of thorns and lilacs, and it is settled that the other side of the path is to continue turfed, and to be planted with beech, ash, and larch."

One reason landscape was so much in the popular consciousness was that in Austen's lifetime the entire English countryside was literally shifting. Acts of Parliament known as Inclosure Acts set out rules to keep people from grazing their animals on common land. Haphazard and poorly managed land strips and trails were replaced with tidy, organized farmlands enclosed by hedges and trees. While this made the land more attractive to people like William Gilpin, it severely curtailed small farmers' efforts to earn a living when they no longer had access to grazing lands for their livestock. The population of Great Britain boomed by about three million from 1750 to 1801, and with this growth in population came many changes.

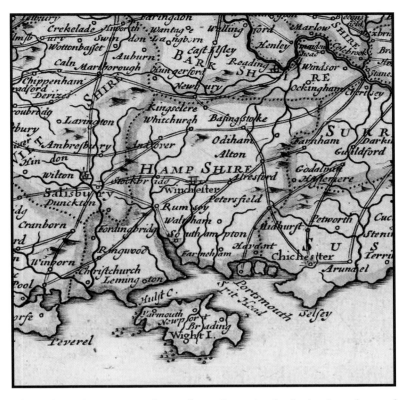

*This eighteenth-century road map shows the routes developing in and around the Austens' home county of Hampshire.*

The Inclosure Acts also helped replace rutted cart tracks with a public-road system that linked villages more directly. Although the roads were still prone to mud and travel was still an ordeal at times, the fact that there were roads at all was a vast improvement in country living. The efficient delivery of letters was also improved. News and more current information could now travel faster—a great leap forward in the quality of country life.

As new roads were being made and new maps being drawn across England, Austen's use of landscape in her novels reflected profound changes going on at the turn of the nineteenth century—changes affecting the gentry classes in an English country village, the world she knew best and loved the most.

Settled and secure in herself and her family's place in the village, Austen's writing developed from the wicked characters and brief spoofs of girlhood into the first drafts of three mature novels. Austen's talent was nurtured in the countryside of Steventon, the safe haven where she lived among books and nature and where she had intellectual companionship, paths for solitary walking, and the time to write.

# FOUR

## Dance and Romance

"There were twenty dances and I danced them all," Austen wrote to her sister after a 1798 ball. Twenty-three-year-old Austen had worn a black cap so stylish it was openly admired by a friend and "secretly," she imagined, "by everyone in the room." She had spent part of her time at this ball flirting with a young man she knew named Calland and confided to Cassandra that she teased the man into dancing with her. "I was very glad to see him again," Austen explained, "after so long a separation, and he was altogether rather the genius and flirt of the evening."

Austen was an excellent dancer, and balls were the brightest social event her rural world had to offer. Because the aristocracy would sometimes invite gentry to their parties, Austen got to experience evenings of elegance and wealth far beyond what her modest home life could offer. But even a ball held at the public rooms—a kind of community hall that could be rented for public events—in the nearby village was equally attractive to Austen, since a ball of any kind meant that she got to dance.

Dancing was a physical expression appropriate for girls. Austen, whose only other form of physical exercise was walking, loved to dance. As she once claimed in a letter, "I fancy I could just as well dance for a week together as for half an hour."

English balls in those days included sit-down dinners and live music. As candles flickered in holders around the room, a fire burned in the grate, and musicians played dance tunes, young women in their most attractive gowns would stand on the edges of the dance floor, hoping one of the men in the room would request a dance. The ballroom was like a microcosm of society, a place where the rituals of courtship were played out under elaborate rules and the watchful eyes of society.

One could not strike up even a casual conversation with someone unless there had first been formal introductions. "There was one gentleman, an officer of the Cheshire, a very good-looking young man, who, I was told, wanted very much to be introduced to me," Austen wrote in a letter describing a ball at Kempshot in 1799, when she was twenty-four, "but as he did not want it quite enough to take much trouble in effecting it, we could never bring it about."

THE FIVE POSITIONS OF DANCING.

*This early-nineteenth-century magazine illustration shows not only the popular dance steps of the time but also contemporary country-dance fashions.* (The Hamlyn Group)

*A contemporary engraving of an English country ball such as the one where Austen might have met Thomas Lefroy.*

Young women looked forward to a ball as one of few opportunities to meet and dance with handsome young men. Jane and Cassandra could spend hours discussing what they would wear and who might be attending a dance. The party atmosphere was especially appreciated in the gloom of long winters, when the roads were barely passable and women had to slip their feet into raised wooden contraptions with metal rings on the bottom, called pattens, in order to keep the mud and horse manure off their party slippers.

It was likely at a ball in 1796 that Austen met and was first attracted to a handsome Irishman by the name of Tom Lefroy. He was in the area to stay with his aunt when he and twenty-one-year-old Jane first met. Many historians mark their relationship as Austen's first love—it is at least the first romance documented in her letters.

*One of Austen's first and few known love interests, Thomas Lefroy.*

"I am almost afraid to tell you how my Irish friend and I behaved," Austen wrote to Cassandra after a ball at which she danced with Lefroy. "Imagine to yourself everything most profligate and shocking in the way of dancing and sitting down together." Austen's letter continued on to say that Lefroy was "a very gentlemanlike, good-looking and pleasant young man, I assure you." A certain unfashionable white coat he often wore was his only flaw, as far as the teasing Austen was concerned.

The budding relationship between Austen and Lefroy was not greeted with much enthusiasm by either family. Austen was very close to Lefroy's aunt, Anne Lefroy, who worried that Jane was excessively attached to the young man. Anne knew that Tom's family was counting on him to go far in life, and that they would certainly not approve of marriage to a person without fame or fortune.

The teasing Lefroy heard at his aunt's house led him to flee the scene when Austen came to visit one day. Though he later called on her at her home, it was becoming clear—though perhaps not to Austen—that his heart was not committed to the relationship. Still, Austen persevered, leading her sister to write cautionary letters warning not to get her heart broken.

For her part, Austen claimed not to care for Lefroy but clearly hoped that he loved her. She was of prime marriageable age and could hardly hope for a better match. As Lefroy's time at his aunt's house dwindled away, Austen wrote her sister to say, "I rather expect to receive an offer [of marriage] from my friend in the course of the evening." Then, in a joking tone, she added, "I shall refuse him, however, unless he promises to give away his white coat."

Concerned that he might do exactly what Austen hoped, Anne Lefroy sent her nephew back to Ireland. As much as she loved Jane, Anne could not risk having her nephew make such a poor match. Despite her casual attitude, Austen must have been very upset when the proposal did not materialize. No letters survive to document Austen's feelings about Lefroy's departure. What we do know is that, soon after he returned to Ireland, Austen began a story she called "First Impressions," which would later become *Pride and Prejudice*. Perhaps writing became a useful distraction for her during a difficult time.

During that same year, Austen became a subscriber to a lending library through which she could read the latest novels. In her letters, she uses these novels to make humorous parallels to her own life. "To-morrow I shall be just like Camilla in Mr. Dubster's summer house," she wrote to Cassandra, "for my Lionel will have taken away the ladder by which I came here, or at least by which I intended to get away, and here I must stay till his return." By referring to a scene from a new novel called *Camilla,* Austen made light of the way she and her sister were dependent on others for transportation. In truth, their situation was not a laughing matter but a source of constant frustration.

Sometimes the sisters had to extend a visit at someone's house when they would have rather gone home, simply for lack of horses and an available chaperone. On one of these occasions, Jane wrote to Cassandra about her relief at devising an alternate travel plan so she would no longer have to wait for her brother Henry's appearance, since "the time of its taking place is so very uncertain, that I should be waiting for *Deadmen's Shoes.*" As unmarried women, the sisters were dependent on others and had little control over their own comings and goings. But this situation appeared to be changing for Cassandra.

Thomas Fowle had been one of Mr. Austen's boarding pupils. Mr. Austen had tutored all four of the Fowle brothers. Thomas had lived with the Austens while attending school. When he was twenty-eight years old and already ordained, Fowle returned to Steventon to officiate at the wedding of Jane's schoolmate and cousin, Jane Cooper (the daughter of Mrs. Austen's sister). The extended Austen family stayed close.

During his stay, Tom Fowle and Cassandra became reunited and spent time together walking and talking on the grounds of Steventon. Jane Austen might have figured out what was happening—that she was losing her sister and best friend to marriage. Before he left Steventon, Fowle asked Cassandra to be his wife. She agreed. Austen's older sister was now formally engaged, meaning Jane would be permanently separated from the person she loved the most.

When Cassandra became engaged, Jane was twenty-two years old. It had only been a year since Tom Lefroy had left England. Although she may have been happy for her sister, rather than writing a celebratory poem for Cassandra, Austen perversely composed a Gothic-style lament about lost love. She clearly had mixed feelings about Cassandra's wedding and some disappointment about the prospect of her moving away. But regardless of Austen's reservations, the mood around the family's house was busy and cheerful. There was another wedding to plan.

Jane Cooper was wed at Steventon, and then in January 1797, the Austens celebrated James's marriage. Cassandra was to be next in line, but first the couple

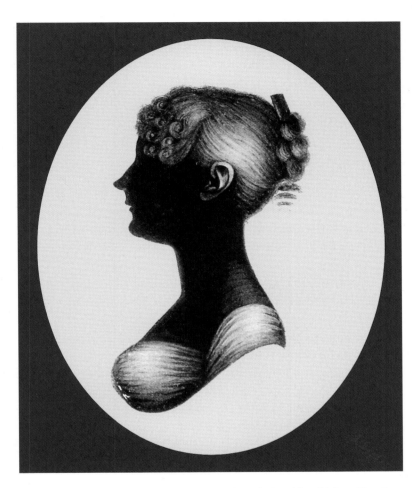

*Jane Austen had an extremely close yet complex relationship with her older sister Cassandra throughout her life.* (Bridgeman Art Library, London)

needed to save up enough money to set up a home. During this time, Fowle was offered an opportunity to serve as ship chaplain on a voyage to the West Indies. The money would help move up their wedding date. Cassandra had enough to keep her busy while the ship

*An excerpt from a chatty letter (1796) to Cassandra, complete with Austen's idiosyncratic spellings, punctuation, and capitalization, focuses mainly on the problem of Jane's going to town with her brother and finding a place to stay while she is there.*

**Rowling Sunday 18<sup>th</sup> September**

**My dear Cassandra,**

This morning has been spent in Doubt & Deliberation; in forming plans, and removing Difficulties, for it ushered in the Day with an Event which I had not intended should take place so soon by a week. Frank has received his appointment on Board the Captain John Gore, commanded by the Triton [Austen means the reverse—the ship is the Triton and its captain John Gore], and will therefore be obliged to be in Town on wednesday—& tho' I have every Disposition in the world to accompany him on that day, I cannot go on the Uncertainty of the Pearsons being at Home.—I wrote to Miss P—on friday, & hoped to receive an answer from her this morning, which would have rendered everything smooth & Easy, and would have enabled us to leave this place tomorrow, as Frank on first receiving his Appointment intended to do. He remains till Wednesday merely to accommodate me. I have written to her again today and desired her to answer it by return of post—On Tuesday therefore I shall positively know whether they can receive me on Wednesday—. If they cannot, Edward has been so good as to promise to take me to Greenwich on the Monday following which was the day before fixed on, if that suits them better—. If I have no answer at all on Tuesday, I must suppose Mary [Pearson] is not at Home, & must wait till I do hear; as after having invited her to go to Steventon with me, it will not quite do, to go home and say no more about it.—

My Father will be so good as to fetch home his prodigal Daughter from Town, I hope, unless he wishes me to walk the Hospitals, Enter

The Story of Jane Austen

at the Temple, or mount Guard at St James [Austen is jokingly suggesting that if left in town she might become a doctor, lawyer, or solider]. It will hardly be in Frank's power to take me home; nay, it certainly will not. I shall write again as soon as I get to Greenwich.—

What dreadful Hot weather we have!—It keeps one in a continual state of Inelegance.—If Miss Pearson should return with me, pray be careful not to expect too much Beauty. I will not pretend to say that on a *first view,* she quite answered the opinion I had formed of her.— My Mother I am sure will be disappointed, if she does not take great care. From what I remember of her picture, it is no great resemblance. I am very glad that the idea of returning with Frank occurred to me, for as to Henry's coming into Kent again, the time of its taking place is so very uncertain, that I should be waiting for *Deadmen's Shoes.*

I had once determined to go with Frank tomorrow & take my chance &cr; but they dissuaded me from so rash a step—as I really think on consideration it would have been; for if the Pearsons were not at home, I should inevitably fall a Sacrifice to the arts of some fat Woman who would make me drunk with Small Beer—[Here Austen is jokingly imagining the terrible fates that could befall her if she dared go into town alone.]

Mary is brought to bed of a Boy; both doing very well. I shall leave you to guess what Mary, I mean.— Adieu, with best Love to all your agreeable Inmates. Donot let the Lloyds go on any account before I return, unless Miss P— is of the party. How ill I have written. I begin to hate myself.

                    Yours ever—J: Austen—


The Triton is a new 32 Frigate, just launched at Deptford.—Frank is much pleased with the prospect of having Capt: Gore under his command.
Miss Austen
Steventon
Overton
Hants

sailed. She went to live with Thomas' family and began sewing her wedding clothes and the household linens she would need to set up a new home. Keeping busy with needlework probably helped her pass the time until her fiancé returned from a journey scheduled to last several months. He would be back at Easter time, and then they would be married at Steventon.

When Fowle's return was only a few weeks away, Cassandra received a devastating letter. Her fiancé had contracted yellow fever and died aboard ship. The news had taken so long to arrive that Cassandra had unwittingly continued to prepare her trousseau for months after he was dead. Fowle had been buried at sea, so Cassandra would not have the ritual of a funeral nor a headstone to mark his grave.

A relative observed that Fowle's death was a blow to the entire Austen family, since the couple had shared such a degree of love and respect. The tragic news saddened everyone in the family. But the one who was hurt the most deeply seemed to bear it with the most stoicism. Austen watched her sister with amazement and respect. In attempting to describe Cassandra's response, Jane told Eliza that her sister managed her grief "with a degree of resolution and propriety which no common mind could evince in so trying a situation." Cassandra has been described as having a somewhat cold manner, and was the kind of person who kept her feelings largely to herself.

For several months, the mood around the household

was subdued. In November, Mrs. Austen took her two daughters to the resort town of Bath, perhaps to distract them from their troubles.

While the timing and circumstances must have made it an understated event, there was in fact one last Austen wedding that took place in December of that year: Henry married his cousin Eliza. Jane's favorite brother had made her favorite cousin an official member of the Austen family.

# FIVE

# Exile

When she was young, Austen got to visit the popular resort known as Bath. She was amused enough by the affected personalities frequently drawn together there, but Austen did not generally enjoy city life.

By the late eighteenth century, most fashionable people knew of Bath, a city built upon natural mineral springs thought to have medicinal properties. People went to Bath on doctors' advice, but most went just for the fun of it. The town was full of amusements. Carriages jingled down cobblestone streets, muffin men and newspapermen hawked their wares, and service carts twisted among thick crowds of people. This din of noise, carnival atmosphere, and the other pleasures of this modern resort provided excitement and escape from the dull

*Austen and her family would have been familiar with this view of the town hall in Bath's busy and modern downtown.* (King George III Topographical Collection, London)

winter hours of country estates. But Austen always preferred the countryside. It was a terrible shock, then, when she learned she was moving to Bath.

The year was 1800, the start of a new century. At twenty-five years old, Austen had a strong, independent mind and a distinct love for Steventon and everything it represented. But one day, when Austen returned home from visiting friends, her mother greeted her with a blunt and stunning announcement: the family was moving to Bath. An Austen family legend claims that upon hearing the news, Jane fainted. Whether she actually did or not, the story underscores her unhappiness about the move. As an unmarried woman, Austen was obliged to follow her parents and make her home with them. She could not afford to support herself as a single woman, nor would it be acceptable to do so if she could. Austen had no choice but to move.

There were several reasons for the Austen family to move. Mr. Austen's health was uncertain, and the springs at Bath promised restorative benefits. He had retired after thirty years of running his parish, and now the position in Steventon was going to be passed on to his oldest son, James, also a clergyman. Since James was the brother Jane was least fond of, she could scarcely rejoice at his good fortune. In fact, she became bitter about it.

Mr. Austen's plan to relocate was startling to Jane but not unusual in the larger social world, since it was something of a trend for clergymen to retire to the city of Bath; it was both popular and affordable. But to Jane, who had no desire to abandon the village life she loved, the idea of living in Bath was abhorrent.

From the time she heard of her parents' plans until the following year, when she had to unwillingly pack and leave, Austen would naturally have vented her unhappy feelings to Cassandra, who was staying at their wealthy brother Edward's estate for much of that time. Whatever those letters contained was likely not pleasant; Cassandra destroyed them.

To leave Steventon, Austen had to part with the farm, the garden, the solitary walks she loved, and the sense of meaning and identity she had formed as a daughter in a family of local importance. In Bath, the Austens would be just another family in a leisure town where people were judged not by intellectual gifts or the degree to which they fulfilled their responsibilities to family and neighbors, but upon the location of their lodgings and the people with whom they associated.

Her father was relinquishing a significant source of income, and the Austens would come to feel the pinch of severe economizing. But for Jane it would be more than merely an economic setback. Austen had every reason to grieve the move. Her father's library, the same influential books she had read, pondered, and discussed with her family, was sold, along with almost every piece of family furniture, because it was too expensive to cart them along to Bath. The sitting room with the patterned wallpaper and chocolate brown carpet where she had spent countless hours in conversation with Cassandra, the hearth at which she had read aloud her first writings and listened to Eliza's stories of French court life, the barn where the Austens had performed their plays—all these would no longer be hers.

Austen was not close to her brother James's wife, Mary, whom she once described as being without a liberal mind. When Jane stepped across the familiar threshold in the future, it would be as a visitor in another woman's home—a woman she did not especially admire or respect. Austen was losing Steventon forever.

In exchange, she was moving to a modern town uniformly composed of cream-colored stone and vast lawns, where summers were insufferably hot and rain was common. In Bath, there were no farms or gardens to tend and just a few trees.

*The Austens moved in across the road from this fashionable social spot called Sydney Gardens, where parties, concerts, and fireworks could be found on a daily basis.* (Victoria Art Gallery, Bath)

*The Pump Room in Bath was enjoyed for the medicinal qualities of the waters as well as for being a popular gathering place.* (Victoria Art Gallery, Bath)

To help residents and visitors fill their hours of leisure, the city of Bath provided parks, walkways, and public rooms, along with entertainments such as bowling, concerts, firework displays, and public breakfasts. There was theater and bathing establishments, but little expression of nature, and none of the functional order found in a village. It would be like living in a postcard.

Cassandra destroyed almost all the letters Jane wrote while she lived in Bath. But the few that remain reveal a woman who had grown irritable and unhappy, and whose sense of humor had become exceptionally cutting. "Another stupid party last night. I cannot anyhow continue to find people agreeable," Austen wrote to Cassandra from Bath. "I respect Mrs. Chamberlayne for doing her hair well, but cannot feel a more tender sentiment. Miss Langley is like any other short girl, with a broad nose and wide mouth, fashionable dress and exposed bosom. Adm. Stanhope is a gentleman-like man, but his legs are too short and his tail too long."

At times during the Bath period, Austen's attitude lost its usual humor. "[I]t gives us great pleasure to know that the Chilham ball was so agreeable," Austen wrote to her sister, "and that you danced four dances with Mr. Kemble. Desirable, however, as the latter circumstance was, I cannot help wondering at its taking place. Why did you dance four dances with so stupid a man?"

In Bath, Austen found herself living among those who lived to impress others with fashion and taste, beginning with the literal elevation of their residence. Lodgings on the hillside were more expensive and more impressive; those near the flatlands by the river were cheaper and without social advantage. The Austen family would begin their time in Bath living at a pleasant hillside street address; but as their reduced income proved insufficient to maintain such lodgings, they were forced, after three years, down the hill to a place they had rejected years before on account of dampness.

Austen's life was confined not only by reduced circumstances but by the society among which she unhappily mingled. The superficiality, the absence of useful purpose, and the lack of trees depressed her spirits. The

Opposite: *This unfinished sketch, painted by Cassandra in 1810, is the only authenticated portrait of Jane Austen.* (National Portrait Gallery, London)

family's strained finances and the lack of cultural stimulation threw a chill upon her creativity. She stopped writing.

While the Bath years were unhappy ones for Austen, there was respite toward the late summer and early fall of each year when her family escaped the heat of town and visited seaside resorts. These escapes afforded her freedom and a change of scene and society.

Her feelings about the seaside might have been deepened by her relationship with a man she met while staying at an ocean-side resort, possibly Sidmouth. According to family legend, the man (his name has not survived) was a bright, interesting gentleman, presumably of the clergy, and quite attractive. Even Cassandra deemed him worthy of her sister and expected the two would marry. He and Jane parted briefly, but not before making plans to meet again. But the next Austen heard of him was in a letter telling of his sudden death.

*The English seaside resort town of Sidmouth, which Austen and her family visited during their years in Bath.* (King George III Topographical Collection, London)

When her holiday was over, Austen returned to Bath, her prospects for happiness bleak. Then, in December 1802, she was offered a chance to leave Bath forever, and to become a rich woman in the bargain.

SIX

# The Proposal

In the fall of 1802, Jane Austen and her sister Cassandra traveled to Manydown Park, an estate owned by the Bigg-Wither family, near their former home at Steventon. The Austen sisters looked forward to a visit with their old friends, the Bigg sisters. What they were not expecting was for the family's eldest son, and heir to the estate, to propose marriage to Jane.

History doesn't reveal how the proposal was offered, but we do know that Harris Bigg-Wither was not big on speeches and that, unlike Austen, he often had trouble finding words when he needed them. At the time he proposed, he might also have had trouble finding an unoccupied room and a moment for privacy. If there were no servants about, perhaps the grandest setting would have been the estate's reception room, entered by a dramatic staircase and lighted by a large bay window that offered a view of the lawns, walkways, and trees on the estate's grounds. If he proposed at the bay window, he might have showcased the prosperity he was offering as part of the marriage pact. In whatever location Harris asked his question, the answer Austen gave him was yes.

It would have been understandable if she had a sleep-less night after agreeing to marry the younger brother of her old friends. Austen certainly had much to contem-plate. She lived in a world where social stations were clear and people knew what was expected of them. In her times, as in her books, it was understood that an English lady of the gentry did not work for a living; her financial security often depended on how well she married. A good marriage improved fortunes and se-cured social status. If a young man or young woman from an upper-class family did not have much money, they aspired to marry someone who did.

The marriage would make her the lady of Manydown. In such a position of wealth, she could provide for her aging parents and Cassandra. She would also gain as sisters-in-law two childhood friends. There would be better gowns to wear, a staff of servants at her disposal, and luxurious living in a region of England she had known and loved all her life.

As Harris's new wife, she would return to this place she loved, only a short carriage ride from her old home. She would be returned to her roots, relieved of her poverty, and rescued from spinsterhood. In those days,

*A wintry view of Manydown Park, Harris Bigg-Wither's family's estate and the scene of the infamous proposal.*

women were typically married before they were twenty-five years old; many took wedding vows in their teens. It was a practical matter to get women producing off-spring when they were young and presumably healthy.

Many women and children died in childbirth. As women aged, their prospects of marriage diminished; society considered single women past the age of twenty-five to be spinsters, women who never married.

Spinsterhood was often perceived as a kind of failure—a failure to attract a man, which meant a lack of feminine allure, and a failure to bear children, which was considered the primary duty and fulfillment of womanhood. Since an unmarried woman past marriageable age frequently evoked pity or scorn, the term spinster was sometimes used in a derogatory manner, and spinsters (perhaps to avoid drawing further attention to themselves) often dressed in rather drab attire—which only served to reinforce the general prejudice that they were sexless or unattractive.

Austen was lucky to be getting any sort of marriage proposal at her advanced age of twenty-seven, and she was not a romantic, especially not at this stage in her life. She would more likely have mused philosophically or even sardonically, upon her situation. After all, her perspectives on marriage were gleaned with the keen eye of a humorist and social critic. Tucked away at home were stories she had written in which all action orbits around courtship and marriage. In her neat handwriting, she had penned the actions of characters who reveal themselves by the way in which they approach matrimony—whether they seek social status, material gain, or even love. How did Austen's situation measure up to the engagements she had created in her fiction?

There is nothing to suggest that Austen actually loved Bigg-Wither, who was six years her junior. And Austen did not likely consider him an equal in terms of mental powers. He did not possess an easy wit and was awkward in expressing himself. They did not have a courtship, nor did they participate in the social rituals that presaged a relationship.

Agreeing to marry Bigg-Wither was a practical move, the kind of decision made by the lesser characters in her novels. The heroines Austen created held out for a marriage based on love and mutual respect, and got plenty of other advantages in the bargain. In a manuscript Austen had titled *First Impressions,* the heroine, Elizabeth Bennet, refuses a marriage proposal from a man who is her intellectual inferior, in spite of the fact that the marriage would have prevented the loss of her parents' home and property. Going against her mother's wishes and the expectations of the times, Elizabeth stands her ground and refuses to marry. In the end she marries for love, choosing a man with whom she has matched keen wits, and whose fortune is enormous.

On this night of her engagement, it would have been natural for Austen to reflect on the state of her feelings, thinking back to that seaside town and the man she had loved and lost only a year earlier. Would she always wonder what might have been? Was this engagement fair to Bigg-Wither? While she might have searched her conscience over whether she could really go through with a marriage to a man not her intellectual equal, she

*She wanted to compose her own feelings and to make herself agreeable to all.*

*This illustration from Austen's* Pride and Prejudice, *the novel that Austen initially titled* First Impressions, *depicts a scene where the book's heroine, Elizabeth Bennet, entertains her friends and potential suitors.* (Courtesy of the Granger Collection.)

might also have taken a hard look at facing an impoverished future if she did not marry.

Whatever went through her mind that night, Austen ultimately acted with the conviction she ascribed to her plucky heroines. The next morning she went downstairs and told Bigg-Wither she could not marry him after all.

Austen's withdrawal from Bigg-Wither's proposal was the social equivalent of a bombshell. It was a shocking announcement, and it meant Jane and Cassandra had to leave Manydown right away. A carriage was called as the sisters hurriedly packed. Soon after Austen delivered her apology, they were on their way to Steventon, where the story would be met first with disbelief and then with reproach. After her aborted affair with Tom Lefroy, Austen had gone and botched another chance at the most important thing a woman could hope to achieve—a good marriage.

The carriage dropped Jane and Cassandra at their old home, where their brother James and his wife Mary now lived. Both the sisters were distraught and crying, want-

*Jane's older brother, Reverend James Austen.*

*Travel by horse and carriage was an unavoidable reality of Jane Austen's times. Although sometimes enjoyable and picturesque, it was more often unreliable and inconvenient.* (Hamlyn Group)

ing to get home as soon as possible. The problem for Jane and Cassandra was that respectable women in those times could not take public transportation without being accompanied by a man. So the only way the sisters could get back to Bath was to convince James to take them in his carriage. It would have been more considerate to have accepted his invitation to stay at the rectory and wait a few days so he could first fulfill his duties at the parish. But emotion apparently pushed them past manners and reason. Very much out of character for either of them, Jane and Cassandra begged their brother to leave with them right away. James agreed, even neglecting his Sunday duties to do so.

Once settled inside the rattling carriage that would take them to the city of Bath, Jane and Cassandra told their brother what had happened at Manydown. For the sisters, the journey was a one-way trip back to a life in Bath that they did not enjoy.

Had Austen made the right decision? She had literally turned down a fortune that day, giving up a life of ease. "To sit in idleness over a good fire in a well-proportioned room is a luxurious sensation," Jane once wrote in a letter to Cassandra. In another letter she wrote, "Kent is the only place for happiness; everybody is rich there." But apparently the promise of luxury and riches was not sufficient reason for her to marry. Until she met a man who was her equal, she would chose to go on as she always had—a single woman and a writer living in genteel poverty.

# SEVEN

# A Place of Refuge

In 1803, England resumed war with Napoleon. The ambitious Corsican (who would soon crown himself emperor of France) began to assemble a large navy. Although it never materialized, for several years the British lived in fear of a French invasion. Two of the Austen men, Charles and Frank, sailed for the Royal Navy. Austen and her family followed their progress intently through news reports and letters.

For someone who had never been in the military, Austen was a keen strategist whose life and stories were peopled with the comings and goings of officers and polite society, all relating somehow to victories and losses. Austen's knowledge of war helped shape the characters and events in her books; it also played a role in her efforts to be published. Jane saw her brothers in

*Jane's fifth brother, Admiral Sir Francis Austen.* (Jane Austen House, Chawton)

uniform prove their competence and advance up the ranks. The only way a writer could do the same was to sell books, to acquire a reading public and the money that came from book sales. "Frank is made," Austen had written joyfully to Cassandra in 1798. "He was yesterday raised to the rank of Commander, and appointed to the *Peterel* sloop, now at Gibraltar." Would Jane Austen be made as well?

While society did not consider novel writing an entirely proper vocation for a lady, it was by far more acceptable to Austen than the lowly job of governess. If her fiction was at least as good as the novels she read, then publication might earn her income. No longer was she the carefree woman who years ago had written humorously to Cassandra, "I write only for fame, and with no view for pecuniary emolument [financial reward]." At this stage in her life, Austen was very interested in getting paid for her work.

# Napoleon

After the French Revolution (begun in 1789), much of Europe feared the spread of the republican beliefs that had sparked a bloody purge of the ruling monarchy. Some rulers, especially in Austria, even suggested trying to restore the French king to the throne. In response, France declared war on Austria in 1792 and executed Louis XVI in 1793. That same year, French violation of a previous treaty provoked England, Spain, and other nations to join the fray. The battles went back and forth until, in 1796, the French seemed to be in trouble when Napoleon Bonaparte rallied French troops to successive stunning victories in Italy.

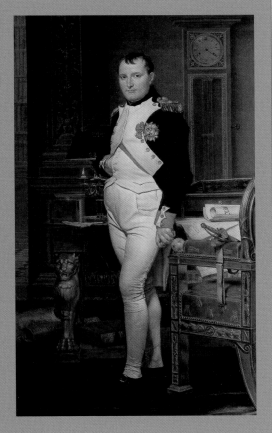

*Napoleon Bonaparte.*

Sardinia submitted, and Austria was forced to sign a peace treaty, but Britain remained defiant—largely the privilege of its geographic isolation.

Napoleon was determined to invade Britain and began to raise a navy, but the great British admiral Horatio Nelson defeated him. Undaunted, Napoleon continued his European campaign, taking Switzerland and Naples, and forcing Austria out of the war. Though the British more than held their own, a temporary peace was made in 1802, at which it was agreed all British triumphs would be returned to France. But war resumed the next year when the British refused to leave Malta, and once again Napoleon made plans for an invasion. Though his hoped-for attack would not succeed, Napoleon did take the crown of Italy in 1805, made an ally of Russia in 1807, defeated Prussia the same year, took Sweden, and put one of his brothers on the throne of Spain in 1808. His military brilliance and fearlessness had made him the conqueror of Europe and brought down the great Holy Roman Empire.

However, in 1812, Napoleon made the ill-fated decision to invade Russia after the czar defied his plan to reorganize Europe's economy. With an army of a half million men, he succeeded in taking Moscow, but the city was left in ruins, and the French did not have the supplies to last out the frigid Russian winter. Napoleon had no choice but to order a retreat, which quickly became a rout. The other countries in the empire he had built turned against him, and he was forced to abdicate just two years later. A brief attempt to retake his crown ended in disaster at the battle of Waterloo in 1815, and Napoleon died in exile in 1821. Thanks in part to the legend of heroism that clung to Napoleon's memory, his nephew would become the emperor of France in 1852, but today Napoleon's legacy is complicated. While he advocated the republican ideals of the French Revolution, Napoleon was also a ruthless warrior who was unafraid to use harsh tactics to repress opposition to his plans.

With the help of her brother Henry, Austen found a publisher interested in her manuscript *Susan*. She submitted the book under the pen name Mrs. Ashton Dennis and received a check for ten pounds in return—not an unsubstantial amount, and enough to encourage her to keep writing.

With this small success as inspiration, Austen began work on a new novel called *The Watsons*. Over the next few years, as *Susan* languished at the printer's, she would focus all her writing energy on this new work.

A death in the family interrupted her work for a while. The Austen family—Jane and Cassandra and their parents—had settled into life at Bath. Though forced by finances into less desirable housing, the Austens were happy enough together. But George Austen's health was not good, and on January 20, 1805, he succumbed to his illness, leaving Jane, Cassandra, and their mother to grieve his absence and then to find a way to make a new life for themselves.

After getting past the initial shock and sadness, the Austen women faced a grim, if inevitable, reality. Without Mr. Austen's pension, which stopped with his death, they would not have enough money on which to live and would be dependent on Jane's brothers for financial support. Though all the brothers promised to help, the women would have to keep a close eye on their finances and move from place to place in search of affordable housing.

During this turbulent time, Austen stopped work on *The Watsons,* to which she would never return. The Austen women relocated frequently for almost two years before finally settling in with Frank Austen and his new wife, Mary. They would stay in the seaside town of Southampton from October 1806 to April 1809. Cassandra spent much of this time with brother Edward in Kent, where Austen wrote to her faithfully, detailing all the activities of her new home and falling back into her usual wry humor. She spent her time helping Mary (especially after Frank returned to sea), entertaining guests, caring for her aging mother, and playing a pianoforte she had scrimped to rent. There were balls, of

*Jane, Cassandra, and their mother stayed in the coastal town of Southampton after the death of Jane's father in 1805.* (The British Museum, London)

course, and Austen still loved to dance, but on the whole Southampton was a trying time.

Thus, it was with mixed emotions that Austen heard the news of her brother Edward's loss. In the fall of 1808, his wife Elizabeth died shortly after the birth of her eleventh child. Jane and Cassandra stepped in to comfort their brother and his children. A few months later, Jane left Southampton for good, traveling with her mother toward their new home—a cottage on one of Edward's estates. After his wife's death, Edward decided to invite his mother and unmarried sisters to live with him permanently. Though he had not helped them sooner, Jane Austen was not going to look a gift horse in the mouth.

*This 1809 oil painting shows the house and church on Edward's estate at Chawton.* (Jane Austen House, Chawton)

For Austen, the move to Chawton Cottage was a homecoming. Only a morning's ride on horseback from Steventon, the new home returned Austen to her old neighborhood and provided her with the security of her brother's protection. There were nephews and nieces to play with, a garden to be planted with her favorite flowers—including lilacs—and the countryside she knew and loved as a child.

Jane, Cassandra, Mrs. Austen, and their close friend Martha Lloyd settled into Chawton, which had formerly served the village community as a roadside inn. It was located where two roads converged en route to London, so travelers passed through frequently. The building itself was so close to the roadside that carriage travelers could look into the dining room windows and observe whoever happened to be at the table. A few months after the women had settled into Chawton, a family acquaintance wrote that she had "heard of the Chawton party looking very comfortable at breakfast from a gentleman who was traveling by their door in a post-chaise about ten days ago."

The women at Chawton, and no doubt every family in the village, were familiar with a few dark deeds associated with the pleasant little cottage. Back when the house was still a public inn, two men had been murdered on the premises (one actually in the road just outside the door, following a fight that had begun inside), and the business was closed down as a result. The two-story structure had remained abandoned until Edward let his steward live there for a time. When the man moved out, Edward fixed the place up for his mother and sisters.

Presumably, Jane and the others didn't mind living in a place where men had once come to drink beer, kill or be killed. It was a home and, for Austen, it was a time of artistic blossoming and self-fulfillment. While she would never have children of her own, she became very close to her nieces and nephews, especially to Edward's eldest daughter, Fanny. Austen delighted in Fanny, who aspired to be a writer and entertained her aunt with stories and romances upon which she sought Austen's advice. That she was the favorite aunt was family legend

*The great house and park at Chawton.* (Jane Austen House, Chawton)

even during her lifetime. Jane, the warmer of the two sisters, genuinely loved children, and was far more willing to play children's games than the coolly reserved Cassandra.

When Edward's family was in residence at the Great House at Chawton, Austen was all happiness. "The pleasure to us of having them here is so great that if we were not the best creatures in the world we would not deserve it," she wrote to her brother Frank. "We go on in the most comfortable way, very frequently dining together, and always meeting in some part of every day."

Austen was cheerful about the six small rooms and the garden in the yard, which was bordered by sweetbriar and roses. She urged the hired gardener to procure syringes, a flower she favored because it was mentioned in one of her favorite poems. Old Mrs. Austen took to gardening again with great enthusiasm, becoming a familiar neighborhood fixture in her green gardening smock. Jane bought a pianoforte and practiced simple tunes to accompany dancing and to entertain the children when they came to visit, rising early to play before breakfast each morning.

Being once more part of a small country village and close to her family, Austen seemed to be deeply contented. She went to a local ball and, afterward, reflected in a letter to Cassandra, "It was the same room in which we had danced fifteen years ago. I thought it all over, and in spite of the shame of being so much older, felt with thankfulness that I was quite as happy now as then." If

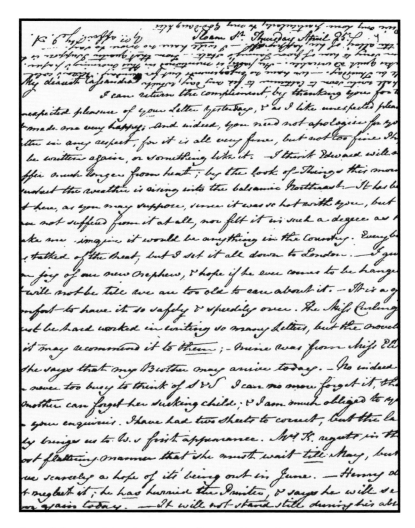

*One of the surviving letters from Jane to Cassandra.* (Jane Austen House, Chawton)

Austen had regained the happiness of years past, part of it was no doubt a result of having gained a secure home that would not be taken from her for nonpayment of rent.

Although she had stopped writing for a little while

after her father's death, Austen had not given up her dreams of succeeding as a writer. Just before leaving Southampton, she wrote to the publisher who had purchased *Susan:* "Six years have passed," she began, "and this work, of which I am myself the authoress, has never, to the best of my knowledge, appeared in print." She went on to demand the publishers either honor their commitment and release the book or return it to her so she could pursue publication elsewhere. The pen name she used (Mrs. Ashton Dennis) gave her the opportunity to end the letter with a clear signature/message: MAD.

In a brief reply, Richard Crosby, the publisher, pointed out that Austen's book had been purchased without any stipulation to publish it. He warned her that if she tried to publish a copy on her own, he would take legal action against her. And if she wanted the rights back, Crosby wrote, the manuscript "shall be yours for the same as we paid for it." Austen swallowed her pride and paid the ten pounds to have her text sent back.

Austen might have lost her battle with the London publisher, but she had not been entirely defeated. Surrounded by the comfort of family and the security of a permanent home, she took once again to her small mahogany table and began writing novels—revising and refining older works and beginning new ones. While she patiently welcomed the frequent interruptions from her adoring nephews and nieces, Austen worked diligently.

She kept her novel writing a secret from many people—including servants and certain relations. Her nephew,

James Edward Austen-Leigh, remembered, "She wrote upon small sheets of paper which could easily be put away, or covered with a piece of blotting paper. There was, between the front door and the offices, a swing door which creaked when it was opened; but she objected to having this little inconvenience remedied, because it gave her notice when anyone was coming." She might have kept it a secret, but the years Austen lived at Chawton Cottage were the most productive of her life.

# EIGHT

# Recognition

J ane Austen was deeply established in the routines
of her life in a country village, yet nevertheless
found herself enjoying a party one evening in London. Her elegant cousin Eliza, now married to Jane's
banker-brother Henry, was throwing one of her lavish
soirees. Austen noted that the elegant rooms were "dressed
up with flowers," and the candlelight was reflected in a
mirror on the fireplace mantle. At seven-thirty that
night, the musicians arrived "in two hackney coaches,
and by eight the lordly company began to appear."
Musicians on harp and pianoforte accompanied professional singers entertaining the sixty-six partygoers.
Among the elegant guests, thirty-six-year-old Austen fit
right in, dressed in stockings of pure silk and a fashionable dress.

During her stay in the big city, Austen had abandoned her drab muslins for more appealing attire. She had also stepped willingly into the many diversions offered by Eliza's vibrant social life—her interesting friends, stylish parties, and teas. Austen seemed to be celebrating a newfound joy, perhaps making up for lost time.

After she mingled with the guests, Austen escaped the stifling heat of the drawing room and slipped into a hallway where she and others cooled off and had the

*This excerpt from an 1811 letter to Cassandra gives the reader a sense of the way Jane Austen's days were spent—there was much time in conversation, much time spent visiting friends, and everyday concerns about shopping, clothing, and money.*

**Sloane St. Thursday April 18.**

## My dear Cassandra

I have so many little matters to tell you of, that I cannot wait any longer before I begin to put them down.—I spent tuesday in Bentinck St; the Cookes called here & took me back; & it was quite a Cooke day, for the Miss Rolles paid a visit while I was there, & Sam Arnold dropt in to tea. The badness of the weather disconcerted an excellent plan of mine, that of calling on Miss Beckford again, but from the middle of the day it rained incessantly. Mary & I, after disposing of her Father & Mother, went to the Liverpool Museum, & the British Gallery, & I had some amusement at each, tho' my preference for Men & Women, always inclines me to attend more to the company than the sight.—Mrs Cooke regrets very much that she did not see you when you called, it was oweing [to some] blunder among the servants, for she did not know of our visit till we were gone.—She seems tolerably well; but the nervous part of her Complaint I fear increases, & makes her more & more unwilling to part with Mary.—I have proposed to the latter that she should go to Chawton with me, on the supposition of my travelling the Guildford road—& *she* I do believe, would be glad to do it, but perhaps it may be impossible; unless a Brother can be at home at that time, it certainly must. . . . I am sorry to tell you that I am getting very extravagant & spending all my Money; & what is worse for *you,* I have been spending yours too; for in a Linendraper's shop to which I went for check'd Muslin, & for which I was obliged to give seven shillings a yard, I was tempted by a pretty coloured muslin, & bought 10 yards of it, on the chance of your liking it;—but at the same time if it should not suit you, you must not think yourself at all obliged to take it; it is

only 3/6 per yard, & I should not in the least mind keeping the whole.—
In texture, it is just what we prefer, but its' resemblance to green cruels
[embroidered cloth] I must own is not great, for the pattern is a small
red spot. . . . I liked my walk very much; it was shorter than I had
expected, & the weather was delightful. We set off immediately after
breakfast & must have reached Grafton House by ½ past 11—, but
when we entered the Shop, the whole Counter was thronged, & we
waited *full* half an hour before we could be attended to. When we were
served however, I was very well satisfied with my purchases, my Bugle
Trimming at 2/4 & 3 pair silk Stockings for a little less than 12./S. a
pair—In my way back, who should I meet but Mr. Moore, just come
from Beckenham. I believe he would have passed me, if I had not made
him stop—but we were delighted to meet. I soon found however that
he had nothing new to tell me, & then I let him go.—Miss Burton has
made me a very pretty little Bonnet—& now nothing can satisfy me
but I must have a straw hat, of the riding hat shape, like Mrs Tilson's;
a young woman in this Neighbourhood is actually making me one.
I am really very shocking; but it will not be dear at a Guinea.—Our
Pelisses are 17/S. each—she charges only 8/ for the making, but the
Buttons seem expensive;—*are* expensive, I might have said—for the
fact is plain enough.—We drank tea again yesterday with the Tilsons,
& met the Smiths.—I find all these little parties very pleasant. I like
Mr S. Miss Beaty is goodhumor itself, & does not seem much besides.
We spend tomorrow evening with them, & are to meet the Colonel &
Mrs *Cantelo* Smith, you have been used to hear of; & if she is in good
humour, are likely to have excellent singing.—To night I might have
been at the Play, Henry had kindly planned our going together to the
Lyceum, but I have a cold which I should not like to make worse before
Saturday;—so, I stay within, all this day.—Eliza is out walking by
herself. She has plenty of business on her hands just now—for the day
of the Party is settled, & drawing near;—above 80 people are invited
for next tuesday Evening & there is to be some very good Music, 5
professionals, 3 of them Glee-singers, besides Amateurs.—Fanny will
listen to this. One of the Hirelings, is a Capital on the Harp, from which
I expect great pleasure.

"advantage of the music at a pleasant distance, as well as that of the first view of every new comer." Austen always enjoyed people watching. If she was feeling happy and confident that night, she had plenty of reason. The year was 1811, and *Sense and Sensibility* was at the printers, waiting to be bound and released as Austen's first published novel.

A lot had happened in the two years since Crosby had returned her manuscript. Once settled in at Chawton, Austen had been encouraged by her family to try once more to find a publisher. On her behalf, Jane's brother Henry contacted a publisher, Egerton's of Whitehall, and urged her to send them a copy of *Sense and Sensibility.*

Revised from an earlier manuscript, *Sense and Sensibility* is the story of two sisters who are very close. The novel centers around the material and romantic struggles of Marianne and Eleanor Dashwood—the former passionate and impulsive while the latter is cool and reserved. Each must take a lesson from the other before things resolve favorably for them both.

The encouragement from Henry helped convince Austen she should not give up. Eliza had always appreciated her wit and talent. If Austen wanted the will to overcome Crosby's rejection and try again, she might recall how her bold cousin had escaped France by her own wit. If Eliza could save her own life, Austen could rescue her literary offspring from obscurity. Egerton's offered to publish *Sense and Sensibility* at the expense of the author. Austen agreed to take the risk.

*This twentieth-century engraving depicts a scene from* Sense *and* Sensibility *in which the major characters stroll in Barton Park, Devonshire. It became very popular to illustrate Austen's works in later editions.* (Courtesy of the Granger Collection.)

Once the deal was struck, Austen's daily life changed dramatically. She spent time in London correcting proofs, attending parties, and ignoring her characteristic frugality by treating herself to new, even fashionable clothes. For a while, she was an entirely different woman from the spinster who left Chawton. She dressed smartly and immersed herself fully in the pleasures of London, feeling some guilt, but not enough to stop the fun.

"I am a wretch to be so occupied with all these things," she wrote to Cassandra, "as to seem to have no thoughts to give to people & circumstances which really supply a far more lasting interest—the society in which you are." Yet Austen went on being "a wretch" and attending parties and teas with Eliza and visiting her cousin's interesting French friends. Once, when paying a social call in London, Austen met an old French count she described to Cassandra in a letter as being attractive and well-mannered; Austen had no way of knowing the man was actually a forger and a spy who would later be murdered by a servant.

Traveling in Eliza's social circles, Austen was mingling with a range of people she would not likely find in her country village, and she was having the time of her life. To Cassandra she boasted of being noticed by a gentleman who observed Austen to be "a pleasing-looking young woman." She added in the letter to her sister, "one cannot pretend to anything better now; [I am] thankful to have it continued a few years longer!" After years of striving, Austen was finally finding a niche for herself.

In the fall of that year, Jane Austen's first book was released in a three-volume set. The title page identified it as having been written simply "By A Lady." Reviewers were favorable, even though they misunderstood the byline and sometimes attributed the book to Lady _____, or "Lady A." The London *Critical Review* observed that the book "reflects honor on the writer, who displays much knowledge of character, and very happily blends a great deal of sense with the lighter matter of the piece." This review came out in February 1812; by summertime, every copy of *Sense and Sensibility* had been sold. Austen was a success.

Despite Austen's publishing triumph, she held fast to

SENSE

AND

SENSIBILITY:

A NOVEL.

IN THREE VOLUMES.

BY A LADY.

VOL. I.

London:
PRINTED FOR THE AUTHOR,
By C. Roworth, Bell-yard, Temple-bar,
AND PUBLISHED BY T. EGERTON, WHITEHALL.
1811.

*The title page of the first English edition of Jane's first published novel,* Sense and Sensibility.

her anonymity, even among some of her family members. When her niece Anna was browsing among the latest novels at the circulating library, she came across a copy of *Sense and Sensibility* and tossed it aside with disgust, saying, "Oh that must be rubbish I am sure from the title."

After her first novel was released, Austen right away went to work revising another of the novels she had first drafted at Steventon. Because someone else had recently written and published a novel called *First Impressions,* the manuscript originally bearing that name became *Pride and Prejudice.* It was the story of the brilliant and attractive heroine Elizabeth Bennet, who engages in battles of wit and principle with the proud Mr. Darcy, whom she initially despises. A complex series of events teaches the two adversaries the value of humility and open-mindedness and they ultimately learn they have more in common than either of them had dreamed possible.

It has been suggested that the character of Mrs. Bennet in *Pride and Prejudice* was fashioned in part after Austen's own mother. In this novel, Mrs. Bennet is always complaining of mysterious ailments, which appear and disappear at strangely convenient moments and never seem to interfere with the prospect of enjoying a fine meal with gusto. This same set of traits is seen also in the character of Mary Musgrove in *Persuasion,* a hypochondriac with "no resources for solitude; and . . . prone to add to every other distress that of fancying herself neglected and ill used." Mrs. Austen, though she lived to the ripe old age of eighty-eight, was well-known for vociferous complaints about her health.

When it came time to bargain over the business of publishing *Pride and Prejudice,* the publisher did not make Austen pay for the printing this time. Based on the success of her first novel, Thomas Egerton purchased the copyright for 110 pounds, and although Austen would have liked to have made more, she was eager to have the money and agreed to the deal.

When the book came out, Austen wrote to her sister at Steventon, "I have got my own darling child from

London." Her authorship was once again a secret; the title page announced that *Pride and Prejudice* was "by the Author of *Sense and Sensibility.*" Very soon after the book was released, the *British Critic* reviewed *Pride and Prejudice,* claiming that the novel was "very far superior to almost all the publications of the kind which have come before us."

A family acquaintance by the name of Miss Benn was visiting at Chawton Cottage when the volumes of *Pride and Prejudice* arrived from London. Austen and her mother pretended not to know who wrote the book, and proceeded to read it aloud to their guest during the course of her visit. Although she was impatient with her mother's reading style (Mrs. Austen did not have her youngest daughter's gift for theatrical reading), Jane Austen was pleased when Miss Benn—the guinea-pig guest—nevertheless liked Mr. Darcy and Elizabeth Bennet.

Miss Benn was not the only admirer. The book was the hit of the season in London, and people were praising it—including a backhanded compliment from one man who insisted that *Pride and Prejudice* was "much too clever to have been written by a woman." When this comment reached Austen through her brother Henry, she no doubt enjoyed a good laugh.

Encouraged by her success, Austen turned to a novel with a more serious tone, featuring a modest, retiring heroine. *Mansfield Park* is her attempt to write a moralistic novel, in which a minister, at first beguiled by an attractive but deceptive woman, comes to his senses and chooses instead to marry the modest and unassuming heroine, Fanny Price. Fanny bears no resemblance to the sparkling Elizabeth Bennet, and her good Christian modesty was not, it seemed, very appealing to readers.

When Egerton saw the manuscript, he complimented its morality, but suspected it would not sell as well as previous books. Competing with novels of scandalous heroines in romantic situations or gothic horror tales, a moralistic tale with a sober heroine would not be a big hit. Egerton did not offer to buy the copyright, but offered to publish the book at the author's expense. Not one literary critic reviewed *Mansfield Park.*

The kind of feedback Austen received from friends and family suggested that her experiment in moralistic novel writing was not a big success. Even her nieces weren't exceptionally fond of the characters.

Austen's next book, *Emma,* is the story of a wealthy and overindulged young woman who tries her hand at matchmaking. Her miserable failures lead her to quit trying to pair others, but not before she stumbles upon an unexpected but perfect match for herself.

For *Emma,* Austen, with Henry, approached a new publisher, John Murray, who struck a hard bargain. While Austen was in London to take care of the details for the printing, Henry fell seriously ill. Austen diligently nursed him back to health and, while Henry was sick, took up negotiations with Murray herself. By now, Jane's writing had become an open secret, and she resigned herself to give up trying to stay anonymous.

One of the medical men attending to Henry during his sickness was Dr. Matthew Baillie, who was also physician to the prince regent, the future King George IV. Probably owing to Henry's inability to keep his sister's identity a secret, Baillie knew Jane was an author. On one of his visits to the house, Baillie said the prince so greatly admired Austen's writing that he kept a set of her books in each of his places of residence.

When word reached the prince that Austen was in London, he sent his librarian to call on her and invite her to visit his library, which she did. The librarian men-

## The Regency Period

King George III ruled Britain from 1760 to his death in 1820. After suffering several nervous breakdowns, by 1810, at the age of seventy-two, he became permanently insane. The last years of his reign were presided over by his son, the prince regent. The prince was famously uninterested in moral uprightness or correct social behavior, and his dissolute ways set the tone for the rest of society. He was

*The Prince Regent, later George IV.*

also a generous patron of the arts, and his regency oversaw the work of the great Romantic poets, including John Keats, Lord Byron, and Percy Bysshe Shelley. But his extravagant spending and the mistresses he flaunted earned him the scorn of much of the population, and Jane Austen was among those who disapproved of his lifestyle. After his father's death, the prince became King George IV. He ruled another ten years and then died in 1830. He was succeeded by his brother, William IV.

The Romantic poetry that blossomed during the regency period is highly focused on the individual and his experiences, shying away from the structure-bound works of the earlier classical period. Romantic poets often wrote about nature and celebrated emotion over reason and feeling over intellect, as in the Keats poem below. The untimely deaths of three of the most significant Romantic poets further adds to their mystery and, for some, their allure. Keats succumbed to tuberculosis at the age of twenty-five, and Shelley drowned a month before his thirtieth birthday. Byron was the comparative elder of the group, dying of a fever at thirty-six.

## WHEN I HAVE FEARS THAT I MAY CEASE TO BE

When I have fears that I may cease to be
Before my pen has glean'd my teeming brain,
Before high-piled books, in charactery,
Hold like rich garners the full ripen'd grain;
When I behold, upon the night's starr'd face,
Huge cloudy symbols of a high romance,
And think that I may never live to trace
Their shadows, with the magic hand of chance;
And when I feel, fair creature of an hour,
That I shall never look upon thee more,
Never have relish in the faery power
Of unreflecting love;—then on the shore
Of the wide world I stand alone, and think
Till love and fame to nothingness do sink.

John Keats

tioned to her that if Austen should like to dedicate her next novel to the prince, she had his permission.

It was a great honor, coming from a prince who admired literature and the arts, but since Austen didn't care for the prince's personal habits (they were vulgar

*A ledger entry by Austen's publisher, John Murray, recording to whom presentation copies of* Emma *should be sent. The Prince Regent's name appears second on the list.* (National Library of Scotland)

*This silhouette, thought to be of Jane Austen, appeared in the second edition of* Mansfield Park. (National Portrait Gallery, London)

in her estimation), she decided to ignore the suggestion. Henry and Cassandra, however, urged her to comply, convincing her that this offer of permission was in fact a royal command. Dutiful Jane Austen made the dedication, and in December 1815, *Emma* became her fourth published novel.

For a woman fated to genteel poverty who had never traveled more than fifty miles from the place she was born, Jane Austen had now tasted luxury, adventure, and

*A late-nineteenth-century illustration of a scene from Austen's 1813 novel,*
Persuasion. (Jane Austen House, Chawton)

freedom. No doubt she would want more of each.

Back at Chawton, Austen began working on another
novel, *Persuasion*—the most mature and most reflective
of all her completed books. In this novel, heroine Anne

Elliot and her beloved Captain Wentworth are parted by the interference of a family friend, a woman who deems the match unsuitable. As Austen always granted her heroines the happiness fate had denied her, Anne meets up with her beloved after years of estrangement, and the two—after a few false starts—are reunited and (presumably) live happily ever after. Jane Austen's life would not have such a fairy-tale ending. Already, she was experiencing the symptoms of the illness that would cut short her life and her writing career.

# NINE

## Journey to Winchester

Since the publication of *Sense and Sensibility* in 1811, Austen's life had become a whirlwind of activity. However, her newfound excitement did not keep her from finding joy in the simple pleasures of life with her family. Over the years, they wrote and visited each other frequently, celebrating marriages and births and coming together to mourn their dead. Austen was particularly saddened by the death of Henry's wife, their cousin Eliza, in 1813. The couple had given her much support and encouragement over the years.

When Austen's own health began to fail, she took comfort in the love and ministrations of her nieces Fanny and Anna. As always, her relationship with her sister Cassandra—though it had its rough spots—was deep and sustaining. But even her family's love could not

*Cassandra painted this watercolor of a favorite niece of Jane's, Fanny Knight.*

ward off the worsening symptoms Austen exhibited, and her health was not helped by continued financial strain. Despite having some money from the sale of her books, Austen could do little to help when Henry's bank failed in 1816. Many small businesses went bankrupt in the economically difficult postwar years. Henry and his investors lost everything—even his servant, Madame Bigeon, lost her savings. But in his typical fashion, Henry was quick to rebound from this disaster and, following in his father's footsteps, joined the clergy in December of the same year.

Meanwhile, Austen's illness continued. No one was certain what ailed her then and no one knows today. In 1964, the *British Medical Journal* published a speculative assessment of Austen's condition based on excerpts from letters that describe the progress of her disease. The diagnosis of Addison's disease would account for most of her symptoms (including constant fatigue, weakness, vomiting, diarrhea, and changes in her skin's pigmentation), but other researchers argue cancer could have been the cause. Addison's is a treatable disease today and is caused when the adrenal glands (located near the kidneys) do not produce enough of certain hormones. Its most distinctive feature is dark spots on the patient's skin.

It was Austen's intention to work for as long as she was able, and she kept at a new novel, *Sanditon,* for some time. She had help from her nieces, but eventually she became too sick to continue. Her surviving letters from

*The first page of what is now known as* Sanditon, *the novel Austen left unfinished at her death in 1817.* (King's College Library, Cambridge, England)

this time show her handwriting reduced to a faltering cursive, a sure sign of muscle weakness and general fatigue.

Austen appeared to hold out hope that she might recover. She wrote to a friend, "I am getting well again, and indeed have been gradually though slowly recovering my strength for the last three weeks. I can sit up in bed and employ myself, as I am proving to you at this present moment." Two days later, a carriage was summoned to take her to Winchester, where she would see the surgeon Giles Lyford.

Cassandra rode inside with Jane while Henry and their nephew William accompanied them on horseback. It was a rainy, dismal day, and the miles of rutted roads severely tested Austen's stoic good humor. Though she had recently described herself as "a very genteel, portable sort of invalid," the trip was taxing.

As the Austen carriage and horses made their way toward Winchester and the hoped-for cure of Jane's malady, there was at least the assurance that Austen might do well to escape Chawton for a while. After all, Austen was not only getting a change of scenery but also leaving behind the routines of home and the inevitable presence of her mother.

Jane was always respectful of Mrs. Austen, despite the fact that the two were not exceptionally close. Even as she suffered, Austen made sure the couch was always available to her mother. For herself, Jane arranged cushions placed on three straight-back chairs—a kind of makeshift couch. There she rested, as well as she could, during her illness.

Austen admired people who could bear suffering with some degree of cheerful stoicism. But if anyone could see through her determined cheerfulness, it would be the one who knew her best—her sister. From inside the carriage, Cassandra could watch the rain and adjust her sister's wraps, making sure Austen did not get chilled.

Finally reaching Winchester, the sisters took rooms on College Street, lodgings that suited Austen. From her bedroom window she could gaze on the dramatic spires of Winchester Cathedral. A bow window in the drawing room looked upon a flower garden. Austen heard the

*This sketch shows the façade of the College Street house in Winchester where Austen was taken during her illness and where she ultimately would die.*

clatter of street sounds and found enjoyment in the change of place; the attentions of her family, including funny letters from her niece Fanny; and visits from her brothers. (The only one of her siblings who did not visit Austen while she was sick at Winchester was her brother Frank—there is no explanation for his absence.) To have her siblings near her, especially, meant a great deal to Austen. "Children of the same family, of the same blood, with the same first associations and habits," she wrote in *Mansfield Park,* "have some means of enjoyment in their power, which no subsequent connections can supply."

Her family's support appeared to have a positive effect on her health, but Austen had still taken the precaution of preparing a will. She left some money to bankrupt Henry and thoughtfully included a sum for his servant Madame Bigeon. Everything else, minus her funeral expenses, was left to Cassandra. Austen kept the will a secret, and kept a brave smile on her face.

Under Lyford's care, Austen's health did seem to improve. Hopeful messages were sent home to the family. On July 14, Mrs. Austen wrote to a family member, "I had a very comfortable account of your Aunt Jane this morning. She now sits up a little. Charles . . . saw her yesterday and says she looked better and seemed very cheerful." Four days later, Jane Austen was dead.

In her last conscious hours, Austen knew she could no longer believe, or pretend to believe, that she would recover. When Cassandra asked her sister if there was anything she wanted, Jane replied that she "wanted nothing but death." Austen was suffering great pain, and among her last words were, "God grant me patience. Pray for me. Oh, pray for me."

Lyford gave Austen something to ease her pain. Cassandra sat next to the bed and supported her sister's head with a pillow for six hours. When she was too tired to continue, her sister-in-law took over. Cassandra returned to sit with her sister, who lived only about an hour more. "There was nothing . . . which gave the idea of pain in her look," Cassandra wrote of Jane's final moments. "But for the continual motion of the head, she gave me the idea of a beautiful statue [and] even now in her coffin, there is such a sweet serene air over her countenance as is quite pleasant to contemplate."

Cassandra took a last look at her sister before her body was taken away. At the time, women did not usually attend funerals (because it was assumed they would become too emotional), so Cassandra stayed in the house while the Austen men followed Jane's casket to Winchester Cathedral.

Although Winchester is well-known for being the final resting place of many important people, for the Austen siblings it was simply an honorable and convenient place to bury their sister's remains. They knew also that their sister had long admired the dramatic architecture of Winchester. Inside the cathedral they buried her body in the north aisle of the nave. Cassandra packed up their belongings and returned

*Winchester Cathedral, where Jane Austen was buried. Fans and scholars still make the trip to visit her grave site to this day.* (King George III Topographical Collection, London)

sadly to Chawton, a home that would never be the same.

After Austen's death, Henry published two of her books—*Persuasion* and *Northanger Abbey*. Formerly titled *Catherine, Northanger Abbey* was a revision of an early manuscript in which a naïve and uninformed young heroine learns a painful lesson about trusting people too readily and taking Gothic novels too seriously. These two novels brought the total of Austen's published works to six novels—enough, it turns out, to ensure her literary immortality.

In the introductory remarks to those final publica-

*This letter, from Cassandra to her niece Fanny Knight, was written in the days after Austen's death. The Thursday referred to is the day of Austen's funeral.*

Tuesday 29 July 1817
Chawton Tuesday

**My dearest Fanny,**

I have just read your letter for the third time & thank you most sincerely for every kind expression to myself & still more warmly for your praises of her who I believe was better known to you than to any human being besides myself. Nothing of the sort could have been more gratifying to me than the manner in which you write of her & if the dear Angel is conscious of what passes here & is not above all earthly feelings, she may perhaps receive pleasure in being so mourned. Had *she* been the survivor I can fancy her speaking of you in almost the same terms—there are certainly many points of strong resemblance in your characters—in your intimate acquaintance with each other & your mutual strong affection you were counterparts.

Thursday was not so dreadful a day to me as you imagined, there was so much necessary to be done that there was not time for additional misery. Every thing was conducted with the greatest tranquility, & but that I was determined I would see the last & therefore was upon the listen, I should not have known when they left the House. I watched the little mournful procession the length of the Street & when it turned from my sight & I had lost her for ever—even then I was not overpowered, nor so much agitated as I am now in writing of it.—Never was human being more sincerely mourned by those who attended her remains than was this dear creature. May the sorrow with which she is parted from on earth be a prognostic of the joy with which she is hailed in Heaven!—I continue very tolerable well, much better than any one could have supposed possible, because I certainly have had considerable fatigue of body as well as anguish of mind for months back, but I really am well, & I hope I am properly grateful to the Almighty for having been so supported. Your Grandmama too is much better than when I came home.—I did not think your dear Papa appeared unwell, & I understand that he seemed much more comfortable after his return from Winchester than he had done before. I need not tell you that he was a great comfort to me—indeed I can never say enough of the kindness I have received from him & from every other friend.—I get out of doors a good deal & am able to employ myself. Of course those employments suit me best which leave me most at leisure to think of her I have lost & I do think of her in every variety of circumstance. In our happy hours of confidential intercourse, in the chearful family party, which she so ornamented, in her sick room, on her death bed & as (I hope) an inhabitant of Heaven. Oh! if I may one day be reunited to her there!—I know the time must come when my mind will be less engrossed by her idea, but I do not like to think of it. If I think of her less as on Earth, God grant that I may never cease to reflect on her as inhabiting Heaven & never cease my humble endeavors (when it shall please God) to join her there.

In looking at a few of the precious papers which are now my property I have found some Memorandums, amongst which she desires that one of her gold chains may be given to her God-daughter Louisa & a lock of her hair be set for you. You can need no assurance my dearest Fanny that every request of your beloved Aunt will be sacred with me. Be so good as to say whether you prefer a brooch or ring.

God bless you my dearest Fanny. Believe me most affectionately Yours,

Cass Elizth Austen

Miss Knight,
Godmersham Park,
Canterbury.

tions, Henry wrote that Winchester Cathedral "in the whole catalogue of its mighty dead does not contain the ashes of a brighter genius." He might have been speaking from a grieving brother's heart, but he was not alone in his sentiments. Rudyard Kipling would later summarize in verse the feelings shared by countless of her admirers:

> Jane lies in Winchester
> Blessed be her shade;
> Praise the Lord for making her
> And her for all she made;
> And while the stones of Winchester—
> Or Milsom Street—remain,
> Glory, love and honour,
> Unto England's Jane.

# TEN

## Legacy

In her lifetime, Jane Austen never made a fraction of the riches her works have generated for others—including those who produced her books as films, those who have merchandised her words on plaques and t-shirts, or those, like the castle owners in Scotland, who sell first editions of her books to collectors. Through most of her adult life, Austen had to guard every cent. "Before I say anything else," Jane began a letter to Cassandra, "I claim a paper full of halfpence on the drawing room mantelpiece . . . I chuse to have my due, as well as the Devil." Austen's poverty, which marked the second half of her life, took a significant toll on her mental and physical well being.

Because she did not choose to marry for money, and in part because, as a woman of the gentry, she was not allowed to pursue a professional career, Austen tried to make as much money as she could from her book sales. "I am very greedy and want to make the most of it," she wrote to a niece. "People are more ready to borrow and praise than to buy . . . and though I like praise as well as anybody, I like what Edward calls 'Pewter,' too."

The impoverished life she'd chosen she considered the lesser of two evils. "Anything is to be preferred or endured," Austen once wrote, "rather than marrying without affection." So she preferred and endured an impoverished spinster's life, and amused herself greatly by writing novels.

Austen worked without formal training, going strictly by her own intuition and following her muse without restraint. "I think I may boast myself to be, with all possible vanity, the most unlearned, and uninformed, female who ever dared to be an authoress," Austen once explained. She was perhaps being coy in trying to dis- courage a fan (who bears a strong resemblance to the foolish Mr. Collins in *Pride and Prejudice)* who wanted her to compose a romance with a plot of his devising. She went on, "I could not sit seriously down to write a serious Romance under any other motive than to save my life, & if it were indispensable for me to keep it up & never relax into laughing at myself or other people, I am sure I should be hung before the first chapter. No— I must keep to my own style and go my own way; and though I may never succeed again in that, I am con- vinced that I should totally fail in any other."

*Austen's niece Anna Lefroy followed in the footsteps of her Austen aunts. Both a painter and a writer, Lefroy would later publish an edition of the unfinished manuscript,* Sanditon.

With a formal education that ended at the age of twelve, Austen knew that even without Latin and Greek, "the greatest powers of the mind" might be nevertheless displayed in a novel. While making readers laugh, she put forth some very serious statements in her novels, especially in defense of women. "Men have had every advantage of us," Austen wrote in *Persuasion,* "in telling their own story. Education has been theirs in so much higher a degree; the pen has been in their hands. I will not allow books to prove anything." But novels were another story altogether; here was the literary venue where a woman could speak up for herself, and where Austen would reveal opinions she would not voice at any social gathering in the neighborhood.

Austen also used her novels to poke fun at history books and the writers of history—all of whom were men. The writing of history is meant "for the torment of little boys and girls," she explained in *Northanger Abbey.* "Though I know it is all very right and necessary, I have often wondered at the person's courage who could sit down on purpose to do it."

In those institutions of higher learning, from which Austen and all other women had been excluded for centuries, men and women now study her novels as part of the college and university course work in English literature. Students write papers about her books. Doctoral dissertations examine her writing and her life.

Austen's literary status in this century might have astounded her, though she might have appreciated that it did not come overnight. Just one year after her death, Cambridge University Library determined that the works of Ludwig van Beethoven and Jane Austen were not important. During the half-century following her death, only one complete set of Austen's works were published.

"Seldom has any literary reputation been of such slow growth as that of Jane Austen," wrote her nephew, the vicar James Edward Austen-Leigh, in 1869. In his memoir of his aunt, Austen-Leigh noted that in earlier years, had anyone in his family claimed that she was among the great authors of her day, it would have been considered mere boasting. But, writing fifty-two years after her death, Austen-Leigh pointed out that Austen's eye for character was such that "Archbishop Whately, in his review of her literary works," put her in "the highest place . . . classed with those who have approached nearest, in that respect, to the great master Shakespeare."

Clearly it was not only the Austen family that saw genius in Jane's works, and it was not only her family that was interested in recalling her life or reading her letters. The public wanted to learn more too. Austen-Leigh's memoir was so much in demand that he published a second edition the next year.

In the early 1900s, an increasing number of those who read and admired her works began to seek out Austen's grave, making pilgrimages to her resting place. The plaque over it described her as a virtuous Christian

# Austen the Miniaturist

While she has come to be praised as one of the greatest novelists in the English language, Jane Austen was always modest about her own work. She usually compared herself to a miniaturist, one who labors over tiny pictures often no larger than a playing card. Although she meant the comparison modestly, she did reveal one of the aspects of her novels that have allowed them to survive for two centuries. Like the painstaking miniaturist painters, Austen's works shine in their attention to detail and description. Most of her works are developed around a variation of the same theme: how young women of her time navigated the perilous waters of courtship to make—or lose—a good marriage. Generally classified as comedies, or comedies of manners, her novels embody the lighthearted attitude with which Austen faced all the events of her life. However, they are lifted above the usual romantic novels of her, and our, time by their wise, gentle humor and deep insight into human behavior. She wrote about what she knew, which was only a small corner of the world, but with such wit and appreciation that audiences today are still able to respond to her work with enthusiasm.

but said nothing of her being an author, so that even a staff member at the church where she was buried did not know of her accomplishments. In the 1950s, bewildered by the increasing number of guests, the man who provided janitorial services inside Winchester Cathedral one day said to a visitor, "I am often asked [where Jane Austen's grave is]. . . . Can you tell me if there was anything special about that lady?"

Some historians have suggested the Austen family wanted to keep Jane's authorship a secret after her death (although by the printing of *Emma,* Austen herself had given up trying to remain anonymous); others speculate that the family either did not recognize the extent of Austen's literary genius or did not wish to have her remembered as a novelist, since it might infer she was a disgrace to the family honor. Eventually, with the proceeds from sales of the memoir by Austen-Leigh, a new plaque was purchased and installed at Jane's grave. It almost begrudgingly acknowledges her as a writer, but like the original plaque, it emphasizes her religious virtues above her literary ones. Nowhere on the plaque did the family mention the novel, a genre that to this day is not entirely without stigma; instead the plaque simply reads: "JANE AUSTEN, known to many by her writings, endeared to her family by the varied charms of her character and ennobled by Christian faith and piety."

The engraved wording goes on to quote New Testament scriptures and, decorated by Biblical images, stands as one of many family remembrances that depict Austen as being more saintly than she saw herself. "Seldom, very seldom," she wrote in *Emma,* "does complete truth belong to any human disclosure; seldom can it happen that something is not a little disguised or a little mistaken." The writer might have penned herself a more candid epitaph. "Pictures of perfection," Austen once wrote to her niece, "make me sick & wicked." Much of the darker and perhaps more revealing records of Austen's thoughts and feelings were destroyed with the letters Cassandra burned.

And yet enough of her life and work remains to intrigue each generation in its turn.

While Austen's novels had a steady following of admirers during the rest of the 1800s, it was not until the 1900s that her popularity began to increase. Beginning in 1932 with the first movie version of *Emma,* millions of dollars have been spent and earned by those who have made Austen's novels into films for television and theater. In the U.S., *Northanger Abbey* has been commercially filmed once, *Mansfield Park* twice, *Persuasion* three times, *Pride and Prejudice* seven, and *Emma* eight times.

*Sense and Sensibility,* filmed for television three times, was made into a major motion picture for the first time in 1995. A renowned British actress, Emma Thompson—also a talented writer and an avowed Jane Austen fan—wrote the screenplay. The public response to the film was phenomenal; the movie grossed over $134 million. The popularity of the movie is interesting considering that many critics consider *Sense and Sensibility* Austen's weakest novel.

One of Austen's great strengths as a writer is that her insight into human nature is as universally shrewd and insightful today as it was in her day. When an American economic advisor was interviewed for a National Public Radio broadcast in 2002, he was asked about the forces resulting from the merging of two computer technology corporations. The advisor suggested that the best way to understand the psychology of corporate mergers

*A promotional movie poster for Emma Thompson's immensely popular 1995 version of* Sense and Sensibility.

would be to read the novels of Jane Austen. She knew a great deal, after all, about those marital contracts that increased fortunes on both sides and secured elevated social positions.

As she lay in her sick bed, Austen scribbled a few lines of poetry. She made no claims to being a poet, but dashing off humorous verses to get a point across was a long-standing family tradition. In the poem, she referred to St. Swithun, a local saint who was honored with a day of celebration. Austen has St. Swithun return from the dead and proclaim:

*This painting of Jane Austen, based on Cassandra's watercolor sketch, was made after her death when Austen became an increasingly popular literary icon.* (Courtesy of Getty Images.)

When once we are buried you think we are dead
But behold me Immortal!

Jane Austen wrote these lines only days before her death. Perhaps she hoped they would be true for her as well.

# Jane Austen's Family Tree

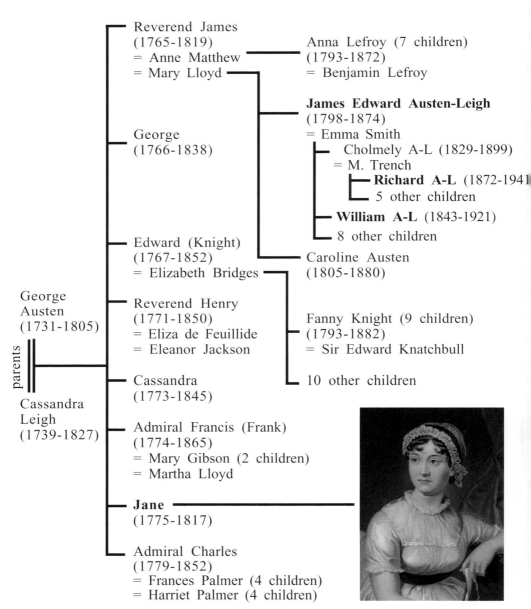

George Austen (1731-1805)

parents

Cassandra Leigh (1739-1827)

Reverend James (1765-1819)
= Anne Matthew
= Mary Lloyd

Anna Lefroy (7 children) (1793-1872)
= Benjamin Lefroy

**James Edward Austen-Leigh** (1798-1874)
= Emma Smith
— Cholmely A-L (1829-1899)
= M. Trench
— **Richard A-L** (1872-1941)
— 5 other children
— **William A-L** (1843-1921)
— 8 other children

George (1766-1838)

Edward (Knight) (1767-1852)
= Elizabeth Bridges

Caroline Austen (1805-1880)

Reverend Henry (1771-1850)
= Eliza de Feuillide
= Eleanor Jackson

Fanny Knight (9 children) (1793-1882)
= Sir Edward Knatchbull

Cassandra (1773-1845)

10 other children

Admiral Francis (Frank) (1774-1865)
= Mary Gibson (2 children)
= Martha Lloyd

**Jane** (1775-1817)

Admiral Charles (1779-1852)
= Frances Palmer (4 children)
= Harriet Palmer (4 children)

**James Edward Austen-Leigh** is the author of *A Memoir of Jane Austen: And Other Family Recollections*. **William Austen-Leigh** and **Richard Arthur Austen-Leigh** are the authors of *Jane Austen: A Family Record*.

# Timeline

1775   Jane Austen is born on December 16.

1776   American Revolution begins.

1785   Starts at the Abbey School.

1787   Returns home, her schooling finished.

1789   French Revolution begins.

1793   Nieces Anna (daughter of Austen's eldest brother, James) and Fanny (daughter of her brother Edward Knight) are born.

1795   Writes first draft of *Sense and Sensibility*.

1796   Writes first draft of *Pride and Prejudice.*

1797   Cassandra Austen's fiancé dies.

1798   Writes first draft of *Northanger Abbey* (then titled *Susan*); James Edward Austen-Leigh is born (he will later write a memoir of his famous aunt).

1801   The Austens move to Bath.

1802   Harris Bigg-Wither proposes.

1803   *Susan* is purchased for publication.

1805   George Austen, her father, dies.

1809   Jane, Cassandra, and their mother find a permanent home at Chawton; purchases *Susan* back from publisher, who had never printed it.

1811　*Sense and Sensibility* is published; the regency of the future George IV begins.

1813　*Pride and Prejudice* is published; Austen's sister-in-law and cousin Eliza dies.

1814　*Mansfield Park* is published.

1815　*Emma* is published.

1816　Henry's business goes bankrupt.

1817　Austen begins work on a new novel, *Sanditon;* dies on July 18.

1818　*Persuasion* and *Northanger Abbey* are published posthumously.

1820　George III dies; George IV becomes king.

# Sources

## CHAPTER ONE: A Rectory Childhood

p. 12, "We now have another girl . . ." David Nokes, *Jane Austen: A Life* (New York: Farrar, Straus and Giroux, 1997), 51.

p. 15, "My poor little George . . ." Ibid., 42.

p. 16, "If Cassandra's head . . ." Ibid., 83.

p. 22-23, "It whines and it groans . . ." Ibid., 63.

## CHAPTER TWO: A Comic Writer

p. 25, "The banns of marriage . . ." Nokes, *Jane Austen*, 96-97.

p. 26, "Beware of swoons . . ." Ibid., 121.

p. 26, 28, "You express so little . . ." Jane Austen, *Jane Austen's Letters,* ed. Deirdre Le Faye, 3rd ed. (New York: Oxford University Press, 1995), 34.

p. 33-34, "a work in which . . ." Jane Austen, *Northanger Abbey* (New York: E. P. Dutton & Co. Inc., 1934), 22.

p. 34, "Where people wish . . ." Ibid., 89.

p. 34, "Expect a most . . ." Austen, *Letters,* 74-75.

p. 34, "There! I may now . . ." Ibid., 28-29.

## CHAPTER THREE: A Home in the Country

p. 36, "We shall have . . ." Park Honan, *Jane Austen: Her Life* (New York: St. Martin's Press, 1987), 48.

p. 40, "We have got *Fitz-Albini* . . ." Austen, *Letters,* 22.

p. 41, "not to consist only . . ." Ibid., 26.

p. 41-42, "She might have . . ." Ibid.

p. 42, "a rector [such as . . ." James Edward Austen-Leigh, *Memoir of Jane Austen* (Oxford, UK: Clarendon Press, 1926), 11.

p. 42, "You know all . . ." Ibid., 9.

p. 44, "Our improvements have . . ." Austen, *Letters,* 51.

**CHAPTER FOUR: Dance and Romance**

p. 47, "There were twenty . . ." Austen, *Letters,* 29.

p. 47, "secretly by . . ." Ibid., 30.

p. 47, "I was very glad . . ." Ibid., 29.

p. 48, "I fancy I could . . ." Ibid., 30.

p. 48, "There was one . . . bring it about," Ibid., 35.

p. 51, "I am almost afraid . . . assure you," Ibid., 1.

p. 52, "I rather expect . . ." Ibid., 3.

p. 53, "To-morrow I shall . . ." Ibid., 6.

p. 53, "the time of its . . ." Ibid., 12.

p. 58, "with a degree of . . ." Austen-Leigh, *Jane Austen,* 105.

**CHAPTER FIVE: Exile**

p. 65-66, "Another stupid party . . ." Austen, *Letters,* 85-86.

p. 66, "[I]t gives us great . . ." Ibid., 72.

**CHAPTER SIX: The Proposal**

p. 78, "To sit in idleness . . ." Austen, *Letters*, 56.

p. 78, "Kent is the only . . ." Ibid., 28.

**CHAPTER SEVEN: A Place of Refuge**

p. 80, "Frank is made . . ." Austen, *Letters*, 32.

p. 80, "I write only for . . ." Ibid., 3.

p. 86, "heard of the Chawton . . ." Nokes, *Jane Austen,* 360.

p. 88, "The pleasure to us . . ." Austen, *Letters,* 215.

p. 88, "It was the same . . ." Ibid., 157.

p. 90, "Six years have . . ." Ibid., 174.

p. 90, "shall be yours . . ." Ibid., 175.

p. 91, "She wrote upon small . . ." Austen-Leigh, *Memoir of Jane Austen,* 102.

**CHAPTER EIGHT: Recognition**

p. 92, "dressed up with flowers," Austen-Leigh, *Memoir of Jane Austen,* 183.

p. 92, "in two hackney . . ." Ibid.

p. 96, "advantage of the . . ." Ibid.

p. 97, "I am a wretch . . ." Ibid., 180-181.

p. 98, "a pleasing-looking . . ." Ibid., 186.

p. 98, "one cannot pretend . . ." Ibid., 186.

p. 98, "reflects honor on . . ." Nokes, *Jane Austen,* 389.

p. 99, "Oh that must be . . ." Ibid., 391.

p. 100, "no resources for . . ." Jane Austen, *Persuasion* (New York: E. P. Dutton & Co. Inc., 1922), 30.

p. 100-101, "I have got my own . . ." Austen, *Letters,* 201.

p. 101, "by the Author . . ." SHOULD THIS BE CITED?

p. 101, "very far superior . . ." Nokes, *Jane Austen,* 400.

p. 101, "much too clever . . ." Ibid., 404.

**CHAPTER NINE: Journey to Winchester**

p. 112-113, "I am getting well . . ." Austen, *Letters,* 340.

p. 113, "a very genteel . . ." Ibid.

p. 115, "Children of the same . . ." Jane Austen, *Mansfield Park* (New York: E. P. Dutton & Co. Inc., 1922), 194.

p. 115, "I had a very comfortable . . ." Nokes, *Jane Austen,* 517.

p. 116, "wanted nothing but death," Austen, *Letters,* 344.

p. 116, "God grant me patience . . ." Ibid.

p. 116, "There was nothing . . ." Ibid., 345.

p. 120, "in the whole catalogue . . ." Honan, *Jane Austen,* 406.

p. 120, "Jane lies in Winchester . . ." Rudyard Kipling, "Jane's Marriage" http://www.kipling.org.uk/poems_jane marriage.htm (accessed September 28, 2005).

**CHAPTER TEN: Legacy**

p. 121, "Before I say anything . . ." Austen, *Letters,* 209.

p. 122, "I am very greedy . . ." Ibid., 281.

p. 122, "People are more . . ." Ibid., 287.

p. 122, "Anything is to be . . ." Ibid., 280

p. 122, "I think I may boast . . ." Austen, *Letters,* 306.

p. 122, "I could not sit . . ." Ibid., 312.

p. 124, "the greatest powers . . ." Austen, *Northanger Abbey,* 22.

p. 124, "Men have had the . . ." Austen, *Persuasion,* 200.

p. 124, "for the torment of . . ." Austen, *Northanger Abbey,* 88.

p. 125, "Seldom has any . . ." Austen-Leigh, *Memoir of Jane Austen,* 135.

p. 125, "Archbishop Whately, in his . . ." Ibid.

p. 126, "I am often asked . . ." Honan, *Jane Austen,* 407.

p. 127, "Seldom, very seldom . . ." Jane Austen, *Emma* (New York: E. P. Dutton & Co. Inc., 1950), 381.

p. 127, "Pictures of perfection . . ." Austen, *Letters,* 335.

p. 131, "When once we are . . ." Nokes, *Jane Austen,* 2.

# Bibliography

Austen, Jane. *Emma*. New York: E. P. Dutton & Co. Inc., 1950.
——. *Jane Austen's Lady Susan*. New York: Garland Publishers, 1989.
——. *Mansfield Park*. New York: E. P. Dutton & Co. Inc., 1922.
——. *Northanger Abbey*. New York: E. P. Dutton & Co. Inc., 1934.
——. *Persuasion*. New York: E. P. Dutton & Co. Inc., 1922.
——. *Pride and Prejudice*. Philadelphia: G. W. Jacobs & Co., 1920.
——. *Sanditon*. Boston: Houghton Mifflin, 1975.
——. *Sense and Sensibility*. New York: E. P. Dutton & Co. Inc., 1933.
Austen-Leigh, James Edward. *Memoir of Jane Austen*. Oxford: Clarendon Press, 1926.
Austen-Leigh, William and Richard Arthur Austen-Leigh. *Jane Austen: Her Life and Letters A Family Record*. New York: Russell & Russell, 1965.
Hodge, Jane Aiken. *Only a Novel: The Double Life of Jane Austen*. New York: Coward, McCann & Geoghegan, 1972.
Honan, Park. *Jane Austen: Her Life*. New York: St. Martin's Press, 1987.

Kaye-Smith, Shelia and G. B. Stern. *Speaking of Jane Austen.* New York: Harper, 1944.

Lane, Maggie. *Jane Austen's England.* New York: St. Martin's Press, 1986.

Myer, Valerie Grosvenor. *Jane Austen: Obstinate Heart.* New York: Little Brown, 1997.

Nokes, David. *Jane Austen: A Life.* New York: Farrar, Straus and Giroux, 1997.

Wilks, Brian. *The Life & Times of Jane Austen.* 2nd ed. London: Reed, 1978.

# Web sites

**http://www.pemberley.com/**
An online home for self-described "Jane Austen Addicts."

**http://www.jasna.org/**
The Jane Austen Society of North America is devoted to the study and appreciation of Jane Austen's works.

**http://www.jane-austens-house-museum.org.uk/**
The house where Jane Austen wrote most of her books is now a museum. Chawton is open to visitors and showcases the furniture and lifestyle of the Austen family.

**http://www.janeausten.co.uk/**
The Jane Austen Centre at Bath is dedicated to describing how Austen's time in that town influenced her writing.

**http://www.pbs.org/empires/napoleon/**
The online companion to the PBS series about Napoleon features lots of information and pictures.

# Index